IS IT JUST ME OR IS
EVERYTHING
SHIT?

ADULT EDITIONS OF CHILDREN'S BOOKS
G * ALPHA MALES * BIG BROTHER VIDEOS
IE'S TEETH * BRITISH JOURNALISTS WHO
END OF SEX AND THE CITY * CAFÉS THAT
SIVE AMOUNTS FOR A MUG OF SHIT TEA
BRITY PRODUCT RANGES * CHE GUEVARA
H BILLBOARDS WITH TRENDY MESSAGES
CAL RELAXATION ALBUMS * COMPLAINTS
CYNICISM * DAILY MAIL * DESIGNER BABY
S * DVDS WITH ADVERTS YOU CAN'T SKIP
S * FAITH SCHOOLS * FAST FOOD CHAINS
VES AS 'HEALTHY' * FILM STARS * GLOBAL
TICS * HENMANIA * HIGH-PROFILE LOCAL
HIP HOTELS * HOMOPHOBIC CHRISTIANS
IKEA * IRAQ WAR EUPHEMISMS * DOM JOLY
ALAH * KEANE * KITSCH TAT SHOPS * LOFT
GEORGE LUCAS * MEDIA STUDIES * KATE
G * NOVELISTS WRITING ABOUT CURRENT
NIS ENLARGEMENT EMAILS * POWERPOINT
LADDER * PUBS PLAYING 'MELLOW DANCE
SFELD * SHOPS THAT PLAY SHIT MUSIC AT
MART CASUAL' * 'STAR' JOURNALISTS WHO
ND BOWLS AS IF THEY WERE THE SCIENCE
CAL EDITOR * TATTOOS * TENNIS PARENTS
AST * UBIQUITOUS FOOTBALL SPONSORSHIP
BIE WILLIAMS * BENJAMIN ZEPHANIAH . . .

IS IT JUST ME OR IS EVERYTHING SHIT?

THE ENCYCLOPEDIA OF MODERN LIFE

STEVE LOWE AND ALAN McARTHUR

TIME WARNER
BOOKS

TIME WARNER BOOKS

First published in Great Britain in November 2005 by Time Warner Books
Reprinted 2005 (four times)

Copyright © 2005 by Steve Lowe and Alan McArthur
Additional material copyright © Dorian Lynskey,
Scott Murray, Joanna Simmons

The moral right of the authors has been asserted.

A CIP catalogue record for this book is available
from the British Library.

ISBN 0 316 72953 1

Typeset in Palatino by M Rules
Printed and bound in Great Britain by
Clays Ltd, St Ives plc

Time Warner Books
An imprint of
Time Warner Book Group UK
Brettenham House
Lancaster Place
London WC2E 7EN

www.twbg.co.uk

IS IT JUST ME OR IS EVERYTHING SHIT?

THE ENCYCLOPEDIA OF MODERN LIFE

A

Adult editions of children's books

If you must follow the adventures of a public school con-juror, even though you are a) notionally a grown adult, and b) have probably been to university or at least to 'big school', why attempt to conceal the fact behind a different cover, as if fellow passengers will assume after a casual glance that you're actually reading Thomas Mann in the original German?

Just because the train on the front is black and white rather than bright red, it doesn't suddenly become a harrowing Booker prize-winner called *Harry Potter and the Genocide in Rwanda*.

How do the dinner party conversations go?

'What are you reading at the moment?'

'It's called *The Very Hungry Caterpillar*. It's about a caterpil-lar who gets really hungry – he just has to keep on eating stuff.'

'I've read it. Marvellous.'

'Oh, don't tell me how it ends!'

'No, I wouldn't. But it's . . . well, it's pretty moving. Oh look, I'm hogging all the Hula Hoops . . .'

Adventurers/mountaineers/explorers

BONG! This is the news: some bloke with more money than sense has got himself lost on a small dinghy in the middle of the Pacific Ocean. Sorry, when I said 'news', I actually meant 'waste of everyone's time'.

The world being largely explored now, is there really any need for a load of posh blokes to try to reach the South Pole living only on roasted peat and using equipment they bought in the Blacks sale? (Note to any posh blokes reading this: that's a rhetorical question – that is, no, there is no need for a load of posh blokes to try to reach the South Pole living only on roasted peat and using equipment they bought in the Blacks sale.) If they do set out over the Pacific in an 8-foot dinghy, risking almost certain drowning, would it be unreasonable to suggest that when they do capsize, rather than expect a multi-thousand-pound rescue operation and media furore, they could at least have the decency just to drown, quietly?

These posh weirdies say things like, 'If you make a mistake in that situation, you're dead.' Well, don't do it then, you twat! Because it's at least feasible that you'll make a mistake! Also: 'If the weather closes in, you're dead.' Well, forgive me, but isn't that what the weather does in the mountains? 'At that point, the weather started to close in!' Of course it did. You were climbing up a fucking mountain.

As recreated in the acclaimed documentary *Touching the Void*, mountaineer Joe Simpson and Simon Yates decided to be the first to climb the treacherous west face of the Siula Grande in the Peruvian Andes. What happened? They made a mistake and the weather closed in.

Simpson fell badly, breaking his leg and forcing the bone through his kneecap causing unimaginable agony. Then, after

Simpson fell over a precipice, Yates, thinking his partner dead, cut the rope and his friend fell 100 feet into a crevasse. Pulling down the rope, Simpson realised he was alone and almost certain to die. At this point he cracked and started punching the ice wall, yelling: 'STUPID STUPID STUPID CUNT! CUU-UUNT!!! STUPID CUNT! STUPIIIIDDD!!! CUUUNNNTTT!!'

A moment of clarity which, all things considered, he might have had in his living room in England. The stupid cunt.

Advice slips

In what meaningful sense does a receipt from a cashpoint constitute advice? All it says is: 'You haven't got any money.' That's not advice.

It would only be advice if they said: 'My brother's just won some money on a horse. I expect he'd lend you a couple of quid until you get paid.' Or: 'If you turned up to work on time occasionally, maybe you'd get promoted and we would-n't have to go through this pathetic charade every month.'

'Cash machine' is also a misleading term: it sounds like an amazing mechanical device for the production of free money. It's not though.

Airport parking

In 2003, a quarter of the profits of the British Airports Authority, which is the authority for airports (in Britain), came not from flying fabulous flying machines in the sky but from parking slightly less fabulous motor cars on the ground. I've no idea where the remaining three-quarters came from, but for the sake of argument, let's say it came from those motorway-service-station-style shops selling SAS/chick-lit novels and sunglasses.

BAA don't even run the car parks – subcontractors like NCP do that, and are also making a fat profit, leaving British airport parking the most expensive in the world.

You could go by train, of course – but the Heathrow Express, crowned mile for mile the most expensive railway journey in the world when it opened, is also owned by BAA, and I don't think you ever hear people sitting round on the Heathrow Express saying things like: 'Ooh, this Heathrow Express is cheap, isn't it? Isn't it cheap?' No, because it is very expensive.

It's not as if it could even be called strenuous, the airport parking game: you just paint a few lines on some tarmac and then let people park on it. Major expenditure? The occasional bit of fence and some cones.

Here is the text of a conversation with a BAA executive that never in fact happened:

US: Hi, I'm Quentin Farqua-Farquason from the Bank de Bank, Zurich, Europe. I understand you have some land that you're just parking cars on and we'd like to invest our riches in you and see them grow, making us all even richer than we are already, ha, ha, ha. How about we build you an hotel on the land, entirely free of charge?

THEM: Thanks for the offer but nah: we'd have to, like, clean sheets and stuff. And frankly we can't be arsed. We're making money hand over bastard fist as it is, mate, for doing precisely shag all.

US: A big shop?

THEM: Fuck off. You've got to, like, order stock. And then people keep coming in and out rendering the place untidy, and you have to order more stock, and keep count, like, all the time. We don't have to do jack fanny-adams. We did paint some white lines once – but that was ages ago. We're parked up on easy street next to a meter that shits gold. Check the address on my card: BAA (Parking Cash-A-Go-Go Division), Offices Plush De Plush, Easy Street, The Maldives. We're flying high.

US: No puns.

THEM: The sky's the limit.

US: Stop it.

Alpha Males

Does your boss sprawl over his chair like he's got two prickly pineapples for testicles? Does he clearly consider murder when faced with a promotion competitor? Does he prowl around believing all female employees are mere seconds from dragging him to the bogs for a short, sharp bunk-up? If so, he probably considers himself an 'alpha male': the kind of business/politics top dog who treats everyone else as his bitch – like the Marquis de Sade with a flip chart.

It's amazing how many people swallow this stuff – that a man's at his best when he's at his most animal – despite the seemingly obvious fact that we are, in fact, humans. In his doomed US presidential election campaign in 2000, Al Gore was implored by image consultant Naomi Woolf to discover the brooding sex panther within. In 2004, John Kerry had to go out and shoot at ducks. If this process accelerates, we'll soon be choosing our leaders by getting two beefy Nazis to have a willy-bashing contest in a pit.

Dominance hierarchies in the animal kingdom were discovered in the 1920s by Norwegian scientist Thorleif Schjelderup-Ebbe. Studying flocks of hens, he noticed how each member recognised its place above and below its peers; the upper echelons got first dibs at the corn (hence the phrase 'pecking order') and peace generally reigned. Clever hens, thought Thorleif Schjelderup-Ebbe.

But applying the same concept to *Homo sapiens* isn't that clever – unless we want our leaders to do head jabs at their opponents' faces before squatting down in the corner for a crap (actually, that might be interesting). In fact, most alpha males are a brain-rotting liability. Look at that Big Bad Wolf of recent British politics, Alastair Campbell, a man so virile he could inseminate a lump of coal. As Downing Street press secretary, he must have reckoned that his rugged rudeness meant all lobby journalists, female and male, fancied the arse off him.

When he left – presumably to go drag-racing with Tommy Lee or shark-bashing with Billy Bob – they missed his verbal spankings terribly and only compensated by beating the bollocks out of each other after hometime.

But surely Campbell's alpha male qualifications only ever amounted to graceless egomania, screwed-too-tight menace and the ability to run marathons. You could say the same for Jimmy Saville* and he never moved out of his mum's house.

Before *Big Brother 6* began, Maxwell predicted he would be the house alpha male. By Day 11, he was demonstrating his leaderene qualities by instigating a competition with Anthony to see who could be first to pee in their pants. Wondering what stunt they could pull next, Anthony suggested: 'We could shit ourselves.'

That's where trying to be an alpha male gets you. Think on, Campbell.

* See the 2000 documentary in which Saville was caught on camera reminiscing about tying up troublemakers in the boiler room of his club in the sixties. Surveying the ensuing scene, police officers would apparently say: 'You were a bit heavy with those two.' Owzabout that, then?

Alt-country

Here are some important facts about alt-country-singer-songwriter-boring-bastard Ryan Adams:

1.   Add a 'B' to the start of his name and you get 'Bryan Adams'.
2.   Ryan Adams really hates this first fact.

At one gig in Nashville, an audience member satirically shouted for Bryan Adams's 1985 hit 'Summer Of '69'. Ryan Adams singled out the offender and refused to play another note until he left the venue. He even offered him $30 of his own money as a refund.

It's Bryan Adams I feel sorry for. No one should have to be associated with alt-country.

Arguments between equally objectionable celebrities

When Jordan calls Victoria Beckham an 'evil, conniving cow'.

Or when Jodie Marsh accuses Abi Titmuss of being a 'whore'.

Or when Christina Aguilera attacks Britney Spears, calling her wedding 'trashy' and 'pathetic'.

Or when Britney Spears calls Christina Aguilera 'scary'.

Or when Victoria Beckham calls Jordan 'vile'.

Or when Jordan claims Victoria Beckham has had breast implants.

Or when Jacques Chirac says George W. Bush 'is so stupid it's amazing he can eat stuff'.

Or when Damien Hirst says that Charles Saatchi is 'arrogant' and 'childish' and 'only recognises art with his wallet'.

Or when Donald Trump brands Richard Branson a 'total failure'.

Or when Victoria Beckham chants 'Who Let The Dogs Out?' at Jordan.

Why don't you all just play nicely?

B

Baby name books

Nobody has ever found a good name in a baby name book because most of the entries are things like Hadrian, Dylis, Mortimer and Binky. Oh yes, and Adolf.

The Collins Gem version genuinely points out under the entry for Adolf/Adolph that 'Adolph and the latinised form of the name Adolphus have never been common names in this country and received a further setback with the rise of Adolph Hitler.'

Setback? I'll say.

Baby pics in newspapers

'Hello, I'm a journalist in my early thirties and I have noticed a terribly strange phenomenon called "babies". They really are fascinating creatures which raise a number of intriguing issues. Interestingly, I myself have just produced one of these "babies" and really think you ought to know more about it.

'Honestly, it's incredible! I didn't know what it was like to have a baby, until I had one . . . You're up all night at first, you know. Actually, here's some pictures of me with my baby. Bloody big ones. Pictures, that is, not babies. Babies are quite small.'

The evidence – viz. the fact the human race has not died

out – suggests that, of all the things journalists might usefully gen up on on our behalf, babies are probably not one of them. People do generally seem to know what babies are, and even where they come from.

Sure, if you have a baby you're going to talk about it at work – that is, with your friends and colleagues – but only journalists (and politicians) crap on about the fruit of their loins while undertaking the actual work.

Bus drivers don't do it: 'Single into town? One fifty. Look at this picture of my daughter. She's got her mother's eyes.'

Or bakers:

'So, packet of doughnuts, one sliced loaf, one picture of my new baby.'

'No, not the picture of the baby.'

'I love him.'

Big Brother videos

It's on telly for 170,000 hours, plus *Big Brother's Little Brother* and all the other attendant shows – and you want more of it that you can keep forever and watch at your leisure. You're a fucking freak. If ever anyone needed to be issued with *The Observer Book of Birds* and given an enforced frogmarch through the outdoors, it's you.

Tony Blair

People dislike Tony Blair for varied and sometimes vague reasons. Here, finally, we present The 10 Definitive Reasons Why Tony Blair Is Fucking Rubbish.

1. Ugly Rumours. You can pinpoint the death of rock 'n' roll as a progressive force to the very second the young Tony Blair picked up a guitar and started playing the riff from 'All Right Now'.

2. His magnificent way with members of the public who disagree with him on television Q&As. 'I think if you listened to the case for war you'd find–' he says before repeating his last point, only more slowly. This is Tonyspeak for: 'Look, prole, the reason you don't agree with me is . . . you're thick!'

3. How he speaks about Healing The World (yes, just like Michael Jackson) before enacting a foreign policy that 'heals' the world by either bombing it or selling arms to it. Heal the 'scar' of Africa? He's done such a good job of healing Burnley that everyone's voting BNP – and Burnley's quite small by comparison.

4. The New Age shit that he and his wife go in for: crystals, Carole Caplin, Mayan rebirthing rituals. Look, mate, if we wanted David Icke in charge of the country we'd have said so.

5. His friends. Tony's best mates include: Derry Irvine, Alastair Campbell, Lord Charlie Falconer and Mandy Mandelson – that's, respectively, a pompous egomaniac, a bullying egomaniac, an egomaniac buffoon and an absolute weirdo egomaniac. Bet it's a right laugh down the pub with that lot. Wonder if Blair says: 'Blimey, me and the missus, last night and every night – doing it and doing it and doing it and doing it and doing it!'

6. The way he exhorts everyone to Think The

Unthinkable – unless this means thinking anything he doesn't think himself, which is genuinely unthinkable. What Blair defines as Unthinkable (capital U) are things most of the rest of us think are unthinkable (are you keeping up?). Things that Mr B finds unthinkable (lower case) actually qualify as some kind of Thought Crime. So it's Unthinkable (that is thinkable) to charge tuition/top-up fees to go to university. But it's unthinkable (lower case) to fund education by taxing the wealthy and big business. So, to sum up, Thinking The Unthinkable means Thinking Thatcherite. But Blair can't say that because it would be honest and unpopular. And that would be unthinkable.

7. The fact he drinks mugs of tea at press conferences in order to look 'relaxed' and 'blokey'. Oh, so it's not meant to make him look like a laser-eyed pixie weirdo with a pole up his bum, then?

8. The invention of 'New' Labour. Or, to put it another way, Old Liberal. You have to wonder why Blair joined the Labour Party, considering he hates it so much. Shame he wasn't around for the Whigs' heyday – now there was a party for do-good lawyers who didn't want to change the world much. In fact, it was to avoid voting for them that people started the Labour Party. Now they're saddled with this great bastard. It takes a special kind of chutzpah to call this progress.

9. Because he will go down in history as 'one of the most popular Prime Ministers ever' despite not being as popular as John Major (whoever he was). In 1997, Labour's 179-seat majority was won with

13,517,911 votes – fewer than the 14,093,007 votes John Major won with in 1992 (oh yeah, I remember – he was the Prime Minister!). Blair's 2001 majority of 167 seats was won with 10,724,895 votes, which is fewer than Neil Kinnock's losing total from '92 (11,560,484). And Kinnock a) lost, and b) went 'oh yeah' at an eve-of-election rally like a pissed-up gibbon.

10. The way he thinks he's doing us all a favour. As a young MP, Blair was always moaning about how much his Islington mates were earning while he suffered on an MP's salary. Isn't the point of going into politics to represent other people's interests, not your own? Maybe we should have a whip-round? Oh, look, we've got three buttons and a chewing-gum wrapper with a naughty word written on it. Lovely.

Bling

Louis XIV was big pimping. Imelda Marcos is a powerballin' bee-yatch. Zsa Zsa Gabor? The motherfucking bomb.

By the late 90s, hip-hoppers had abandoned all pretence of fighting the powers that be. Instead, most had become the kinds of cartoon money-grabbing capitalists that could slip neatly into a Soviet propaganda film – except replacing the bushy moustaches and top hats with hos. Once it took a nation of millions to hold them back. Now it takes a nation of millions to hold their coats.

It's now so passé that even *Cosmopolitan* has stopped using it, but the word to describe this phenomenon was 'bling' – a coinage from New Orleans rapper B.G. of the wonderfully named Cash Money Millionaires collective (hmm, definitely a money theme developing here) to describe light glistening in diamonds. His 1999 US smash 'Bling Bling' portrayed a fantastic world of Mercs, platinum rings, diamond-encrusted medallions, helicopters and drinking so much fine booze that you end up vomiting everywhere (bet you didn't know that was cool, did you?).

In a startlingly widespread display of Stockholm Syndrome, the ideal for urban kids suddenly involved transforming yourself from ordinary human into monomaniac money machine. By 2004, the Roc's PR Strategy, a business plan for Jay-Z/Damon Dash's* Roc-A-Fella music/clothing/booze/jewellery corporation was laced with terms like 'mother brand', 'brand equity' and 'product seeding'. Dash described himself as 'a lifestyle entrepreneur. I sell all the time. Whether it's music or sneakers, it's all marketing, marketing, marketing, 24 hours a day. My whole life is a commercial.'

Clearly these new capitalists are better than the old ones, though. They don't get rich off the backs of others – they do it just by being fly. Oh, hang on: ultimate blingster P Diddy – who produces his own custom-made Sean John diamond-encrusted iPods – destroyed his image as a shrewd businessman in December 2003 when confronted by Lydda Eli Gonzalez, a 19-year-old former factory worker from Honduras. She asked him how come the people who made his $50 Sean John T-shirts were paid 24 cents per shirt, were limited to two toilet breaks a day and forced to do unpaid overtime. Puffy said he didn't know anything about it. It's okay, though, he said, he'd look into it and, if what she said were true, he would sever all ties with the factory. Cool.

Although a pay rise might have been more use than unemployment.

For all but a handful, of course, bling is a glaring lie: 50 Cent's 2003 album *Get Rich Or Die Tryin'* should more accurately have been called *Highly Unlikely To Get Rich, Far More Likely To Die Tryin'*. But, as Public Enemy's Chuck D recently claimed: 'Hip-hop is sucking the nipples of Uncle Sam harder than ever before.' What he failed to report was how P Diddy actually manages to suck the nipples of Uncle Sam and his great mate Donald Trump at the very same time. That makes four nipples. But then, as we know, he is quite a guy.

* Dash famously refuses to wear any item of clothing twice, but does it count if he goes swimming? When he gets out of the baths – and presuming he hasn't lost his locker key – does he put his clothes back on, or does he take a box-fresh set with him? And what if he forgot to have a shower? He's just slipping on a nice Thomas Pink shirt when – d'oh! – he realises he smells of chlorine. So he slips off the shirt and his boxers and he has a shower. But when he gets out, does he pop the shirt back on, or does he require a new one? And if he does require a new one and he hasn't got one with him, does he go home in the buff? Or what?

Body art
Actually, I think you'll find it's called a *tattoo*. When Picasso painted *Guernica*, it was not, as I understand it, a toss-up between a nightmarish pyramid arrangement of horrors in black, white and grey representing the effects of fascist bombing, or a big eagle with 'Mum' written underneath it. I could be wrong. (See also **Tattoos**.)

Bookmakers

It is not true what your gran tells you: that no one makes money from gambling and the bookies always win. Very rich people who own horses make money from betting as they have the information and connections to get on to a good thing. It's old men who hang around in bookies all day smoking fags, cheering for horses and dogs in a very quiet, desperate, defeated way, often abbreviating the name as if using the full name of an animal that will, in all likelihood, only cause them pain is just too much for them, who tend not to win.

If bookies look like they're going to lose – that is, loads of people start betting on something that is likely to actually happen – they slash the odds to the point where no one will bother. If that doesn't work, they close the book and stop taking bets. They would call this 'sound business sense'. I would call this 'being a bunch of cunts'.

So it's okay to go in to the bookies and say 'I'll have a tenner on Mystical Dancer in the 2.30. I have it on the excellent authority of a man down the pub that it is a very fast horse indeed, certainly faster than all the other horses in this race, which is, after all, the nub.' And they just say 'Okey-dokey, skip'. At no point do they say 'Mystical Dancer? Cack Dancer, more like. It's a fucking donkey, mate. Save yourself a tenner: unless all the other horses fall over during the race, you haven't got a fuck of a chance. And even then there'd be no guarantee, it's fucking rubbish.' But if you go in and say 'I'll have one hundred of the Queen's pounds on *Big Bag of Bollocks* by Pompous O'Bastard to win the Booker Prize at 66-1' and some bloke in North Shields has done the same, and they think you know something they don't and they might lose a few quid, they say: 'Sorry, mate, 66-1? Oh no, that should have read 1-20 – slip of the pen – and, erm, anyway we've closed the book for fear we might not make loads of money.' Bastards.

Books on CD (except for blind people)*

I may not know much, but I do know this: books is for reading.

Being read is one of the key characteristics of your actual book. If you don't like reading, you're just not the sort of person who wants to get involved with books. And this isn't rocket science: I learnt it in infants' school.

The second most insane example of the audio book is the complete *Ulysses* by James Joyce. Now, this is by no means an easy book. It is a very long book – with long words in it and, famously, a really, really fucking long sentence. Not being a booky type, you may decide it's not for you. Fair enough. But what sort of freak who doesn't wish to read *Ulysses* buys the Naxos 22 CD set of someone else reading it for them? You can't be arsed to read it, but you can be arsed to listen to 22 CDs? Freak.

But the first most insane example is *Finnegan's Wake* (also by Naxos), a book that even people who really like reading get frightened of. Indeed, people who like reading so much they do precious little else, who like it so much they did Double English Literature With Extra Reading at university just so they could do a shitload of reading, have been known to run off down the street when someone produces a copy of *Finnegan's Wake*, shouting 'Stay back! That's too much reading!' For this reason, I firmly believe that all the *Finnegan's Wake* CDs are actually blank.

* This entry is EXCLUSIVE to the print edition of *Is It Just Me Or Is Everything Shit?*. The audio book slags off people who waste time reading when they could just listen to it on CD, leaving their hands free for doing jigsaws and eating fudge.

David Bowie's teeth

People are forever babbling about David Bowie's capacity for reinvention. But he's been playing the role of smirking bread-head for over two decades now so he might want to consider reinventing that for starters.

In the last few years, he's used famous personae to flog Vittel in France; he's larked about with wife Iman for Tommy Hilfiger; and he's belatedly hopped aboard the bootleg mash-up bandwagon in order to plug that fearless avatar of the avant-garde, Audi. He's cashed in his legacy so often it's a wonder he doesn't appear on QVC, hawking non-stick pans dressed as Ziggy Stardust. Many rock veterans are obsessed with cash, but only Bowie has launched his own internet banking service and issued bonds on Wall Street. Not that many people can boast that they're Bowie Bond millionaires. Except, oh, David Bowie – The Man Who Sold Himself.

Bowie's vanity used to manifest itself in dressing like a Martian transvestite. When he started getting his teeth fixed in 1980, he drifted down to the orbit of a daytime soap actor. Is it mere coincidence that he recorded his last great album in, oh yes, 1980?

On 'The Maid Of Bond Street', from his 1967 debut album, Bowie sang of 'Hailing cabs, lunches with executives / Gleaming teeth sip aperitifs', intending it to be a nightmarish vision of soulless urbanites. Now he probably considers it a good day out.

Brand books

'I know, I'll read a book, I'll be educated and amused, I'll laugh, I'll cry, it'll change my life. I'll read a book about Starbucks. By Starbucks. In Starbucks.'

Popular titles currently available include *My Sister's a Barista: How They Made Starbucks a Home From Home* by John Simmons (currently available in Starbucks); *Amazonia: Five Years at the Epicentre of the Dot.Com Juggernaut* by James Marcus (an Amazon bestseller); and *The Perfect Story: Inside eBay* by Adam Cohen (can be purchased via eBay). For adults, this is actually a step down from reading Harry Potter.

How utterly unimpressed with life's infinite possibilities would you have to be to go to Starbucks and read a book about Starbucks, by Starbucks, while having a Starbucks?

If the whole world were decimated tomorrow, except for my house and the nearest Starbucks, and all the reading matter in the world had been destroyed, even, like, all the magazines and stuff, and there was nothing else to do ever, even watch the telly, and I was the only person on Earth except for the people working in The Last Starbucks on Earth, I'd stay in.

Okay, I might pop out occasionally, but I definitely wouldn't read the fucking Starbucks book in fucking Starbucks. Fucking ever.

And I'd steal their milk.

British journalists who never got over the end of *Sex and the City*

There is a certain type of British female journalist who never got over the end of *Sex and the City*. Constantly on the search for her own 'Big'-type suit guy, these are the only people in the world who still go on 'dates'.

You're looking for that ideal guy who knows grooming but is also slightly roughed up; who all the waiters know, who deals stocks and also deals art and respects a woman's independence but will also splash out on something to make you look and feel fabulous at the casino. You do this by filling professionally concerned broadsheets with articles about how rich people are great and how expensive stuff is the best stuff.

Now, it's hard to say how much the series' portrayal of the New York singles scene is fact or fantasy without doing more research – and that, frankly, is not what this book's about – but if you transplant this vision to the thronging metropolitan centres of the UK, well, you're screwed.

Look: all the money-raking bachelors around these parts are a braying bunch of yahoos who simply want to a) finish the gak, and b) come on your face. Sorry about that.

So, while it seems churlish not to wish you luck, please don't get your hopes up. Oh, and if you do ever find your own personal 'Big', do you then think you might possibly be able to shut up?

That would be just so fabulous!

Gordon Brown

At the time of writing, Gordon Brown was still the Prime Minister-in-waiting; a brooding, fat-faced Hercules just itching to clean out all the Blairite crap from the Augean stables.

If we believe the script, he's ready and willing to redirect us to The Promised Land. He's Westminster's own Special One. He's Episode IV: A New Hope. That kind of thing. This is, after all, the man who claimed (at the 2003 party conference) that Labour is 'best when we are Labour', a coded message to the disillusioned hordes meaning: 'Come to daddy.'

But if Labour is at its best when it's Labour, presumably Labour is not at its best when it's doing things like: promising the CBI 'a light touch' on workplace health and safety inspection; or siding with employers against unions in having people work more hours in a week than they are likely to sleep; or letting public sector workforces be subsumed by privatised McJobs; or relaunching the system of PFI, which means your local hospital wing is built by the same company that does school meals in Baghdad and nothing works quite right because everything's done on the shit and which can all be summed up in one word: fucking Jarvis. Okay, that's two words.

So, who was that letting the side down all those times? Two clues: he's the Chancellor of the Exchequer and he's called Gordon. And he's got a fat face. Okay, that's three clues.

George W. Bush

George W. Bush is much vilified for reasons such as wars, oil, incapacity to eat pretzels without causing injury to himself (the freak), abolishing tax for the rich, stuff like that – but his critics miss the central, absolutely key point: the fact that George W. Bush claims to 'speak Spanish'.

Chutzpah? *Holà! Si!* Fucking hell, *si!* You'd think he'd be better mastering one language at a time, and that English would be a more pressing priority. But *no, Señor*.

This Hispanic turn is, of course, politically motivated. Here's how it works. In Texas there are lots of Hispanic voters.

So it helps, if you want to be Governor of Texas, to get Hispanic people to vote for you. So you 'learn Spanish'. It's unclear if 'speaking Spanish' means he can conduct negotiations with Mexican trade ministers in their native tongue. Or maybe just that he can almost ask his way to the swimming pool – if there's also a mike strapped to his back? But still.

As news of his Latin temperament spread, Bush's share of the Hispanic vote rose from around a third in the 2000 presidential election to 44% in 2004. Kerry (whoever she was) still took 53%, but the gap with the Democrats closed from a 36% deficit in 2000, when some bloke stood, to 9% – which, as any seasoned election analyser will tell you, is less. If you did some more sums you could predict by how much Bush would lead in the Latino vote next time if he were allowed to stand, which he isn't, and it would probably make for scary reading, I should expect. *Holà!*

This is why Bush has been sponsoring massive immigration from Spanish-speaking countries – mainly Mexico, which Bush really likes because it rhymes with Texaco, but also Spain itself. That's why Laura delivers leaflets saying 'Come To America' outside Barca games. And why the pair of them often hit the Andalusian coastline to swim naked and free. Which, in fact, now I come to think about it, isn't happening. So, actually, all this stuff about the Spanish thing is wrong and the people who concentrated more on the wars and tax cuts and stuff were right. Sorry.

Buy Nothing Day

The single most pointless pseudo-political protest in the history of the world, short of actually killing yourself in protest about something but not telling anyone that's why you're killing yourself or what you're protesting against. Don't buy something today, buy it next week! That'll bring down the system all right. Grr.

C

Cafés that charge excessive amounts for a mug of shit tea

A pound? A fucking pound? I *know* what tea costs! I make it all the time!

Cafés that charge excessive amounts for a set breakfast but try to justify it by putting a bit of basil on the tomato

I *know* how much basil costs, too! And it's not the £2 you've just slapped on the price of my breakfast. It's much less than that – slightly over £1.99 less. Why don't you just have done with it and move your family into my fucking house?

Cafés that cut sausages in half down the middle

Does *anyone* believe they're getting two sausages, rather than one bad sausage sliced down the middle, with the curved sides pointed upwards to momentarily create the illusion of two bad sausages? Anyone at all?

Cafés that offer you butter but then give you marg

It's the lies I can't stand.

Cafés that refill Heinz/HP bottles with cheaper sauce

You're not fooling anyone.

Jimmy Carr

The real reason that charmless, podgy-faced careerist ex-ad man Jimmy Carr – who is famous for his gut-churningly shite-hawk jokes about women being fat and ugly and is NEVER OFF YOUR FUCKING TELLY – is pathologically unable to turn down work, however nuts-dissolvingly awful it is, is that he single-handedly cares for around 35 elderly neighbours. He pays for all their heating through the harsh winter months and, as soon as he's finished filming, he's off delivering them their dinners with those metal lids keeping them warm.

Not really. He's just a grasping cunt.

Casualty

Far be it from me to let the fact that I haven't seen this pro-gramme since the mid-1990s stop me from pointing out the following differences between this silly, makeweight BBC 'drama' and a real casualty unit:

1. On *Casualty*, the staff aren't all ripped to the tits on stolen prescription drugs.
2. In real life, no casualty unit has ever treated a small boy who's been electrocuted after his kite drifted into electric power lines, let alone an average of three per series.
3. On *Casualty*, they haven't contracted out all their major services to the people who do the cleaning.

What I have seen is *Casualty* spin-off *Holby City*, which is *much* better. The doctors are all called things like Zuben, Rick Griffin and Mr Campbell-Gore, names that could proudly do service for a motorcycle display team or a circus. And everyone's always shagging each other. Now *that's* drama.

Did you ever see *My Hero*, with Ardal O'Hanlan in it? There's a doctor in that, too. Shit, wasn't it? Particularly the bloke who thought he was an alien who used to be in *Bread*. Now that *was* shit. Carla Lane: shit. What was the question again?

CBI, the

Talking in *The Times*, CBI director-general Sir Digby Jones said there was a general perception that 'Everyone hates businessmen'. However, this is not because of businessmen. It's because of the media.

Digby complained that TV programmes like *Blackpool* and *The Office* portrayed managers negatively as 'greedy' or 'bullying'. Digby even complained to ITV about the *Coronation Street* plotline involving a serial killer businessman. When you start seeing Richard Hillman as an agent of anti-boss propaganda, you're clearly feeling touchy about something or other.

In reality, of course, all bosses are lovely. And none are more lovely than Digby Jones. But every time you hear about his organisation, it is in headlines like 'The CBI says more staff appear to be skiving off with faked illnesses', or 'Sickies cost businesses billions, says CBI' or 'The UK's minimum wage should be frozen at £4.85 an hour until 2006, says CBI', 'CBI says CO_2 limits suicidal for competitiveness' or 'CBI demands the retirement age be lifted to 70'.

In summation: the CBI reckons workers are wasters who are always only inches from stealing the computers and shitting in the cupboards. Bosses, meanwhile, are great. So you'd better back off or we'll pick up our balls and fuck off to Taiwan. So, not 'greedy' or 'bullying' at all, then.

It's certainly a moot point what kind of image the modern businessperson Digby Jones believes he is projecting. Hoping to colour in some of the many blanks of this enigmatic figure, we sent a questionnaire to the CBI's Centrepoint HQ asking Digby Jones:

1. The CBI/Real Finance FDs Excellence Awards dinner at a Park Lane hotel in April 2005 – 'a night of celebration of the role of the finance director' – would have cost a business £2044.50 for a table of 12 plus wine, travel, accommodation, etc. Which is over five grand. Prudent spending by business?

2. The morning after the dinner, how many of the guests woke up with a head cryogenically frozen by booze and then called in with a special 'stuffed-up nose' voice? Have you ever done this, Digby Jones?

3. Digby Jones: you are a proud member of the National Trust. But isn't the National Trust just a

load of old communist toss? If stupid old buildings can't pay their own way then they should be
blown up. You're getting soft, man.

4. In the middle of all these corporate galas, regional
    dinners and minor awards ceremonies, do you ever
    think, 'Oh my stars, this is tedious. What am I
    doing here? I'm pissing my life away'? And idly
    dream of the day that man may be free and the
    whole squalid business is replaced by a life of
    beauty and equality and freedom? Or aren't you
    that fucked?

5. Where the bloody fuck do you go to get your hair
    cut, man? You're out there representing the Best of
    British and your hair looks like shite having a bad
    day.

Sadly, Mr 'Stop The Shirkers' never bothered his arse to
reply. Lazy sod.

Celebrity magazines

'She's too FAT!' 'Wait, she's too SKINNY!' 'Or is she so utterly
FANTASTIC it's not true?' 'No, she's a SLAPPER! With sweat-
patches!'

For fuck's sake, at least make your minds up.

Celebrity product ranges

In 2004, spotting a gap in the market for credit cards aimed at
impressionable teenagers, pop sensation Usher launched his

own: 'Hey kids, if you enjoyed my hit album *Confessions*, you'll love a life in debt.'

The hardest-working woman in showbusiness-related products is Linda Barker. How she fits this in, what with spending on average 12 hours a day advertising other people's products, is a mystery: perhaps she's working on a Linda Barker Time Machine? So far, she has put her name to sofas, a Smart car, a special leather-bound *Complete Dickens*, a hairbrush, a range of cats, some pants, a caravan that folds up into a suitcase and an aircraft carrier. She also has an exercise video: *Linda Barker's Simple Yoga*. Really the exercise video was unnecessary as I know lots of people who, when Linda Barker comes on the telly, claim to 'run a mile' – which has got to be better for them than a bit of yoga, overall.

The very acme of shitty celebrity products is the Very Important Product range at Habitat. This range was clearly dreamt up by a mentally disturbed Situationist on Ritalin. Except it wasn't: various celebrities were allowed to 'design' their own product.

This range incorporated the Stirling Moss A4 Stackable Filing Tray; to be fair, they do attain incredible speeds – particularly considering they are only trays. Further items included the Linford Christie shoe box – a wooden box that holds one pair of shoes; so that's pretty useful – and the Sharleen Spiteri CD rack. Anyone owning a Texas CD, however, obviously doesn't like music and will only own two other CDs, both of which will be by Robbie Williams – so what would they need a rack for?

For a grand, you could get a table designed by Daft Punk covered in different coloured light-squares which respond to noise and light up – like a Studio 54-style dancefloor. The only point of this is to say rude words to it and see which squares light up. And you can do that in the shop. They're quite polite in Habitat so it takes about five minutes of you saying 'wee wee-poo poo' and 'cockflaps' to a table before they throw you out. Apparently.

Charity, tits out for

On occasion, all the diseases and disasters, the billions afflicted by worldwide poverty, the endless oceans of distress, the maimed unfortunates desperate for some kind of relief, fill one with the need to help in the only way that's appropriate. That's right, folks, it's bikini carwash time!

This is, after all, a fitting way to raise money for Cancer Research UK. How better to highlight the hardships of all those middle-aged women undergoing intensive radio- or chemotherapy on their breasts than to parade some healthy, pert, soaped-up jubblies around a supermarket car park in Surrey? How very thoughtful you all are.

Nothing moves us to give like a good dose of smut. And so there are charity calendars featuring *Casualty* babes in naughtily revealing medical drapes, Chippendales-style charity thongathons, Macy Gray going starkers. After the World Trade Center attacks, some lapdancing clubs were even moved to lay on special nights collecting money for the families of the victims. Now that's really bending over backwards for others.

So, come on everyone – let's really pull together this year. What about the starving in Sudan? Who's up for a Charity Soapy Tit Wank?

Charity, trips of a lifetime for

There you are, an Inca, sitting on your Trail, appreciating the view and munching on a coca leaf, generally enjoying the atmos, when along come 30 bored computer programmers from Bristol, having the time of their fucking lives 'raising money for cancer'. It's okay, though – it's 'for charity'.

Because charity does not begin at home: it begins on holiday. Previously, people booked a holiday and paid for it themselves. You didn't say to your workmates: 'I fancy two weeks in Ibiza, getting ripped to the tits on Ecstasy tablets and contracting an STD: fancy chipping in? Go on, if you all put in 50 quid I can go for sweet jack nix.'

Now, though, people are quite happy to say: 'Go on, it's only 50 quid and it's for disabled kiddies.' But then they mumble: 'Except half of it pays for me to go camel trekking in Mongolia.' And when you ask them to repeat the second bit louder, they show you a picture of a child who's been blown up by a mine.

Other similar gambits might include: 'If you pay for me to go to the pub tonight, I'll put your change in the charity box – go on, it's for lifeboats, you stingy cunt.'

Some people do pay the travel costs of their charity holiday themselves, but it's still fucked up. Cancer research, care for the elderly, orphaned children: what happened to the idea that society should fund these things, what with it being stinking rich and all? Instead, it's the cue for everyone to start cycling along the Great Wall of China (which, by the way, you can't see from space – that's just a barefaced lie. If irrelevant . . . but still, you can't).

Charles, Prince of Wales

He might believe that cancer can be cured by daily coffee enemas, but the heir apparent does make a nice sausage. Maybe this is because those freely ranging Duchy of Cornwall pigs spend the summer months on the Highgrove estate rolling around in 'cooling mud baths'. Sometimes, when schedules allow, Charles even finds the time to join them (that's after he's stuffed half a jar of Gold Roast up his arse).

Now, some people might say: look, he doesn't exactly make the food himself, he gets some farmhand to do it all for three lumps of coal and an orange at Christmas and what's he doing owning a whole fucking county anyway isn't it the 21st century now he's decided he hates science too the fucking freak and if people shouldn't be getting above their station why doesn't he try a bit of agricultural labouring himself the thick fuck and anyway if he really loved his people he'd give all the biscuits and sausages away for free the usurious cunt. That is what some people might say. But not me. I like the sausages and let that be an end to the matter.

Other than that, though, I haven't got a good word to say about the loony feudal shithead jug-eared parasite bastard.

Che Guevara merchandise

Let's not be negative about this: Che Guevara did help put in power a Stalinoid dictatorship which locks up gays and trade unionists – but, you know, fair's fair, he did also have a cool beard. And Cuba can't be proper Stalinism, like in Eastern Europe, because it's really sunny there, whereas Eastern Europe is cold. Brr.

Che is everyone's favourite facial-hair-motorbike-stood-for-some-stuff-but-I-don't-know-what-it-was-and-don't-really-give-one-check-out-the-beard-man revolutionary. Ace. The sort of revolutionary you can safely put on T-shirts, clocks and candles – yes, Che Guevara candles are available from a firm called Rex International. They also do candles with Elvis on them. Same difference. Che's real name was Ernest which is perhaps not so cool, but who cares when you factor in the whole motorbike thing?

Or maybe the kids really are into vague, trigger-happy yet hippyish developing world guerrilla vanguard revolutionism tinged with Stalinism? Either way, buoyed up by Rex's success, other companies are trying to float similar products, including a chain of North Korean restaurants full of images of Kim Il-Sung (provisionally called Yo! Rice), and a range of sportswear called simply Gulag.

Rex are responsible for Che coasters and the Official Che Guevara calendar. How the red blazes do you get an *official* Che Guevara calendar? Presumably, there is a Guevara estate somewhere sanctioning all this crap? In fact, we've got hold of a tape of the chat between Che's relatives and a Rex representative where the historic coasters decision was made:

AUNTIE FLO GUEVARA: It's what he would have wanted.
UNCLE DAVE GUEVARA: Yes, yes. He was always drinking fluids from glasses and mugs, but not all in one go. He needed something to rest the glass or mug on, so as not to mark the surface of the table.
AUNTIE FLO GUEVARA: He was very considerate like that.
UNCLE DAVE GUEVARA: Yes, he was a considerate boy: he always left his machine gun in the hall.
AUNTIE FLO GUEVARA: Yes. And his motorbike.
UNCLE DAVE GUEVARA: Yes, the motorbike also.

AUNTIE FLO GUEVARA: How much money were you going to give us again?

UNCLE DAVE GUEVARA: Yes, we need to pay our gardener in the Maldives. We haven't lived in Cuba for years – it's shit. They lock up gays, you know.

AUNTIE FLO GUEVARA: Yes, and glasses and mugs – they just put them on the table. Just right on the table: they don't even care if it makes a mark!

UNCLE DAVE GUEVARA: They're animals. Cigar?

Chick-lit

Competition: Three of the below chick-lit titles are real chick-lit titles and two are not real but made-up chick-lit titles. Can you spot the not real but made-up ones? (Answers below.)

1. *Dot.Homme*: Mid-thirties singleton Jess is sent by friends into the world of internet dating – with unexpected results!

2. *The Ex-Files*: Take a soon-to-be-married young couple, four 'exes', mix with alcohol, and stand well back. Boom!

3. *Virtual Strangers*: Fed up, frustrated and fast approaching forty, Charlie suddenly thinks she may have finally found her perfect soulmate – via e-mail!

4. *The Mile High Guy*: Twentysomething Katie is a flight attendant thrown head over heels by a handsome, wealthy first-class passenger. Emergency landing!

5. *Old School Ties*: Tracey is 32, married and bored.

Then she spies an advert for a reality show on a perfect school reunion. Friends – and enemies – are soon reunited!

Answers: sadly, there are no answers.

Chuckle Brothers, The
Disturbing.

Church billboards with trendy messages
In a bid to woo trendy young groovsters inside their doors, churches put up boards bearing messages that incorporate topical events or 'street-yoof' language. But this can be confusing. I once read a billboard saying: 'Jesus is dead good.'

Which, unfortunately, was printed in such a way that casual passers-by would read: 'Jesus is dead. Good.'

'Christianity – less a religion, more a relationship.' But Christianity is clearly more a religion than a relationship. It's the whole weekly meetings giving thanks to an invisible deity at a communal place of worship that gives the game away.

Citybreaks
Spend half your prized three-day break getting there and coming back; struggle to reach your 6:30 a.m. flight at an airport that calls itself London but is actually in Norfolk, to get somewhere that calls itself Venice but is actually in

Switzerland. Then realise you have seen everything in the first hour.

The travel agent literature for Bruges claims: 'Throughout the year streams of tourists photograph its beautiful buildings and wander in and out of the chocolate and lace shops.' As anyone who has wandered in and out of chocolate and lace shops will tell you, it doesn't take very long; and once really is enough. After spinning out your stroll to the point that you hit The Wall and start burning your own body fat, you realise that there's nothing else to do for the remainder of your stay except drink heavily and/or row with your travelling partner.

You might become so desperate for variety that you're persuaded by the guidebook's intriguing descriptions to explore a picturesque suburb where the real city dwellers, possibly even vibrant immigrant communities, live out their lives drinking insanely strong coffee in colourful gambling dens.

On arrival, you find yourself walking down an empty street where the silence is punctuated only by the bark of a dog and the distant chink of cutlery from behind shuttered windows. An old man's vacant stare seems to ask the question that's already forming in your mind, pounding at your forehead: 'What the *fuck* are you doing *here*?'

Classical relaxation albums

No one's interested in listening to classical music for the exciting bits any more. Dark, doomy symphonies evoking a Europe awash with revolution and romantic spirits tussling with their demons, eventually climaxing with some big fuck-off cannons going off all over the place? No thanks, we've only just finished our Tesco Metro dinner. And we've lit some candles.

Beethoven's Symphony no. 9, with its tormented lows and ravishing highs, was all right back in the day. But never in a million years could it fit into a classical relaxation compilation, advertised in the middle of *Des and Mel*, with Andrew Lincoln cooing in weirdly oversensual tones, like he's spent all his voiceover money on exotic candles and jelly: 'Relaxing . . . classical . . . music . . . mmmm . . . mmmmm.'

Silly old Ludwig. If only he'd stuck to that balming rinky-dink stuff that's like sipping a cool glass of yoga, he might have saved himself a whole lot of bother. Shame, because he really must have put himself out. What with being stone deaf and all.

Clone towns

In 2005, researchers at think-tank New Economics Foundation discovered that many high streets in Britain looked the same. Apparently, a number of towns were becoming 'clone towns' in which 'the individuality of high street shops has been replaced by a monochrome strip of global and national chains'.

Okay. And for this they were paid money, were they? Next: think tank reveals that Scotch eggs have got eggs in.

CNN, NBC, etc.

Who would have thought, when the concept of the global media first appeared, that what they meant was the whole globe getting *American* media? Really, *who* could have predicted that?

And why are they always called Bob? The bloke doing the piece to camera in Washington? Bob. Who hands back to the studio – to Bob. Sometimes it's women. But mostly it's Bob.

I once saw this on CNN:

BOB: A flood in Indo- Indo- . . . how do you say that, Bob?

BOB: Inda Indakinesia.

BOB: A flood in Indostania has left 400 people dead with another thousand so far unaccounted for. But first, let's go back to Minneapolis to get an update on that dog up a tree. She's a real cutey, too. Bow wow, Bob.

BOB: Bob. Bow wow.

When I say I 'saw' this, I had been drinking so it might not have happened. In case you were going to use it in an essay or something. Or work as a lawyer for CNN.

They definitely did call forces fighting the US in Fallujah 'anti-Iraqi forces', though. And you can check that. You can't fucking touch me for that one – so don't even try. I was on my holidays. It was August 2004. Not sure which day it was. They had CNN where we were staying. You might wonder what I was doing inside watching CNN when I should have been outside in the sunshine enjoying my holiday. But it was the evening.

Cockney advert babies
Surveys have shown that consumers are most likely to trust

financial advice when it's delivered in a soothing yet sober Scottish accent – somewhat hilariously subverting years of political correctness with the notion that we all see the Scottish as 'careful with money'.

But there's no evidence to explain why viewers should be swayed in their choice of nappy by a doughy infant gruffly overdubbed to sound like one of the blokes who held down Jack the Hat while Reggie brained him. Perhaps the implication is that failure to purchase the right brand will result in your little angel grimly sneering: 'Mug me off with own-brand nappies and I'll open you up, you cahnt'.

But this is a stupid idea. Even if a baby did threaten me, I wouldn't be that bothered. I could take your average baby, no bother – they're fucking tiny.

Dogs are stupid and will happily run around with bog roll in their mouth, but cats are always 'discerning'. The laws of ad-thropomorphism dictate that cats must always sound upper class and sleepily self-satisfied, like Leslie Phillips drinking fine wines in a jacuzzi. They come on like they own half of Mayfair, when in fact they'd fucking starve if you didn't give them mashed up animal genitals out of a tin. Assholes.

Colours of the season

Who actually decides the new colours of the season? Is it God? No, it's not. It's actually a global network of analysts and trend forecasters in organisations like the Color Association of the United States (CAUS) and Pantone Inc. who together form a kind of new black Bilderberg Group. They meet in secret, possibly in Davos, possibly in a hi-tech base built into a volcano, and usually let the weakest link in the group – possibly the one with a distasteful penchant for lime green – take their chances down the shark chute.

Their forecasts influence designers of shirts, paper products, candles, cars, tiles, paints, silk flowers and lipstick. When they say 'Aqua', the rest of the world says, 'How high?' These people know about colour. The CAUS website boasts: 'Pinks and fuchsia were everywhere in spring 2003; CAUS members knew this in spring of 2001.' That's some serious knowledge.

But predicting colours is a strange pursuit – a bit like predicting cows. Basically, they're just kind of there; not really getting any better or worse with the passage of time. This partly explains why, describing their recent aqua-blue ranges, designers Narciso Rodriguez and Michael Kor could only really claim inspiration from seeing – surprise! – some blue water.

'Colour is always out there,' pointed out Leatrice Eiseman, executive director of the Pantone Color Institute, to *Time* magazine. 'We just have to determine where it's coming from at any given time.'

Beware of flying colour. It's 'out there'.

Comedy clubs

In every comedy club chain, the compere always kicks off with the lie: 'We've got a great bill for you tonight.' His ice-breaking banter involves asking the audience where they have come from. Perhaps inevitably, the answers rarely provoke high comedy so the conversation very soon starts resembling distant relatives who haven't met for many years exchanging pleasantries at a funeral: 'So where did you come from?' 'Doncaster.' 'Great.'

The first act begins by explaining that he's 'trying out new material'. Sadly, though, somewhere in his mind the phrase 'new material' has become entirely disassociated with the concept of 'jokes'. Fairly soon, it goes so quiet you can hear people pissing in the toilet.

After a few more minutes of 'no jokes', a stag party starts yelling: 'Fuck off, you're shit.' 'No,' the comedian shouts back, 'you fuck off.' When this has finished, the host returns to try simultaneously to convey the two sentiments 'You were a bit nasty to that chap, don't do that or I'll have to get stern' and 'Please, for the love of God, do not turn on me'.

This pattern is repeated three or four times until the arrival of the headliner – or, rather, the pseudo-headliner, the actual headliner having cancelled (a fact advertised by a small handwritten note stuck on a wall behind a curtain). The stag party's 'fuck offs' will grow in intensity until you realise, as they trade unamusing insults with another bastard working through their 'issues' by inflicting their paper-thin personality on people who have never done anything to hurt them, that you have paid good money to sit in a dark room listening to people bellow 'fuck off' at each other.

Then there's a disco.

'Common sense'

In August 2004, Michael Howard said: 'Whenever there is a conflict between political correctness and common sense, let me tell you where I stand – firmly on the side of common sense!'

This put the rest of us in the difficult position of having to come out against 'common sense'. What with 'common sense' apparently meaning 'hating gypsies'.

And there was me thinking it meant things like not lighting your farts near petrol pumps.

Sofia Coppola

The portrait of the babbling airhead Hollywood star in *Lost In Translation* was reportedly based upon writer/director Sofia Coppola's first-hand experience of Cameron Diaz.

I would personally be very keen to see Cameron Diaz make her directorial debut with a movie that featured a supercilious rich-kid indie *auteur* who does pseudo-profound confections that people initially twat themselves over but which, on second viewing, are the cinematic equivalent of non-flavoured rice cake, with comedy scenes that are not especially funny, endless 'arty' shots of the Tokyo skyline filmed out of hotel windows and dialogue that is only naturalistic in the sense that it possibly took as long to write as to say, and which are considered original only by people who have never set eyes on any other footage showing characters suffering from exquisitely well-turned neon-lit urban ennui like Wim Wenders directing a crap U2 video in 1993.

And she was shit at acting.

Cosmetic surgery gone wrong as televisual entertainment

Permanent scarring: now *that's* television.

Crabtree & Evelyn

Don't even get me started on those bastards.

Crazy Frog

I'm not an idiot and so I do understand that being so annoying is part of the Scandinavian ringtone sensation's appeal for people who like that kind of thing. So, you know, whatever.

My issue is this: why did he have to have a cock?

During the frog reproductive process, the male grasps the female's body in a special embrace called amplexus. The female releases eggs, usually into water, and the male sheds sperm over them from an opening called the cloaca. As no penetration occurs, the male frog has no need for external sex glands.

So. I'll ask the question again: why did he have to have a cock?

Creative industries, the phrase

Funny how you never hear novelists or painters say they work in the 'creative industries', but only squalid little advertising people. How could this be?

J. Walter Thompson, the world's oldest ad agency – founded in 1864, they currently handle Ford and Unilever – tell us on their website: 'We believe: in influencing the world to think more creatively.' Provided, presumably, only if that thought is 'must – buy – more – stuff'.

If you listen to advertisers, you'd think they're the fucking Oracle and that for a fee they'll slip you The Answer. They are obsessed with being seen as 'creative', but what they do seems rather to be 'parasitical': pinching cultural innovations and using them to persuade people that they want stuff. So there's a dilemma right there for us all to think 'creatively' about.

JWT also believe in 'raising the creative bar as far as it will go. Then jacking it up a notch after that.' However, having already raised the creative bar as far as it will go, further notching up the creative bar will cause the creative bar to break. The creative bar will be completely fucked. That's just physics.

J. Walter Thompson further believe: '90% of the world's surface is made up of ideas. The rest is water.' A brief look at an atlas or infants' school geography textbook could have disabused them of this errant fallacy. Creative? Maybe – after all, they have completely made it up. But certainly not 'industrious'.

Leo Burnett (who do Heinz and McDonald's) are also into 'belief': 'We believe Disney, McDonald's, Nintendo, Heinz and Kellogg's are some of the world's most valuable brands because people have gone well beyond merely buying them. These are brands people believe in. When people believe, they buy more, pay more, stick with a brand more and advocate the brand to others. And so belief is the ultimate brand currency.'

Instead of all this gibberish about creative bars and making wine from water, really to convey the essence of their activities they'd all be better off with just one page of flashy swirly graphics, fading in these four words:

We

are

cack

wizards

Critical reassessment

Yes, for fuck's sake. By which I don't mean yes, as in 'the affirmative'. I mean no – to Yes.

In their lifetime, the prog-rockers were critically reviled and were held in particular derision by the punk movement. There was a reason for this: they were so bad they made your ears want to die. However, having tried to wreck completely all music by making really bad music is no barrier to critical reassessment, the process in which rock critics look for a date on a CD, see 1973 and think: 'Hmmmmmmmm, interesting . . .'

The criteria for critical reassessment reflect the high critical standards traditionally exercised by the music press. The criteria are:

- You must once have put a record out.
- Erm, that's it.

You might imagine reissuing Jeff Lynne's *The War Of The Worlds* in a lavish 7-disc box set (including the best club mixes from 1979–2005, rarities, outtakes and a 'making of' DVD) has scraped through the bottom of the barrel into the dark, dirty ground.

But even now a few neglected cases are still, in our humble opinion, ripe for rediscovery:

- Solo albums by members of Roxy Music that aren't Brian Eno.
- Salt-N-Pepa – *The Later Years*.
- The George Martin stuff on side two of the original 1969 release of the *Yellow Submarine* album (which nobody has actually ever listened to).
- The Drifters – *The British Seaside Years*.

- 'I Eat Cannibals'-era Toto Coelo.
- U2.

Culture of cynicism, complaints about the

In recent years our leading public figures have often spoken of the public's need to restore its faith in our leading public figures. We have all, say these wielders of power in politics or industry, been poisoned into believing that everyone who wields any power in politics or industry is a principle-starved bag of poison after as much free booty as they can stash in the voluminous pockets of their extremely expensive overcoats. When, of course, this couldn't be further from the truth.

At the dawn of the century, Tony Blair kicked off the backlash against our sneering ways when he described the Millennium Dome as 'a triumph of confidence over cynicism'. So is the exhortation 'Leyton Orient for Europe'.

On a 2002 visit to Africa, he again attacked 'the cynics back home' who suggested he might not make good on his earlier promise to 'heal the scar of Africa' – when he was definitely going to get round to it 'later'. It was only a matter of time before he whipped open his briefcase to distribute personally cod and chips and a buttered slice to all.

Alastair Campbell, meanwhile, told the Commons' public administration committee that it wasn't his fault nobody believed anything any more; it was the media's 'culture of negativity'. Charles Clarke claimed elements of the press were 'actually about the promotion of cynicism'.

The press hit back with *Daily Mail* columnist Melanie Phillips saying Dr David Kelly's death meant that 'our whole political culture has become putrid with ruthlessness, cynicism and deceit'. (Talking of ruthlessness, anyone questioning her right-wing moral doctrines was standing up for 'nihilism, the worship of the self and gross personal irresponsibility'.) Prince Charles then jumped aboard, calling our pervading cynicism both 'the corrosive acid that eats away unseen' and 'a drug . . . a dangerous substance' (which actually makes it sound quite exciting).

Clearly, relentless negativity is a terrible thing – these people who go on about everything's just a big load of old shit. But being told off for being cynical by that bastard nest of vipers is like being told to put your tits away by Kelly Brook.

Culture of praise, the*

As in, when describing an unremarkable work of artistic creation, the application of words like 'magnificent', 'unbelievable', 'an awesome achievement' and 'If you don't think this is unfathomably great, I'm coming back with my rifle and the two of us are going to teach you some sense'. Are these bringers of hyperbole being paid in sacks of gold? Or are they the subjects' mums in disguise?

According to these throwers of garlands, we live in an unparalleled age where a new masterpiece is being created by another genius roughly every 20 seconds as opposed to, say, every other year. The very week it was announced that *Top of the Pops* would be demoted to BBC2, presenter Fearne Cotton followed a piece about the *Magic Roundabout* film, saying: 'Kylie?! *The Magic Roundabout*?!?!? Genius!!!!' Really? Is this genius as in Leonardo da Vinci? Or better?

If a book reviewer likes a book they've been given, they often claim it is 'hard to put down'. Has anyone else except book reviewers ever noticed this phenomenon? Some books are even 'dare-to-put-me-down' books. Soon we will be faced with 'if-you-put-me-down-I'll-rip-your-fucking-feet-off' books. And then where will we be?

Hanging from awnings outside theatres, a succession of boards cherrypick key phrases like 'awe-inspiring', 'unspeakably moving', 'pure brilliance' and 'a courageous step into the void'. It's surprising audiences aren't struck deaf, dumb or blind by their experiences. At the very least they should have pissed themselves.

Talking of pissing yourself, actresses like Kate Winslet often find themselves referred to as 'brave'. When recently asked by veteran CBS reporter Tom Fenton about being 'an uncompromising, very brave actress', Winslet replied: 'Being brave is very important because sometimes, you know, you can find yourself in scary situations at work, you know, when there are scenes that are difficult to do. And you can't run away from it, so you just have to go headlong into it.'

We must all applaud Kate Winslet's ability to cope with scary situations at work. But, we must also wonder, how brave is she really? It would be intriguing to see how she'd hold up faced with the challenge of, say, a burning orphanage.

Watching her go headlong into that would indeed be 'awesome'.

---

* Dr Jonathan Miller has called this entry: 'Truly stupendous – a work of unparalleled greatness. It actually made me aroused. I'd be very surprised if the authors didn't cure cancer. Just by looking at it.'

D

Daily Mail

The *Mail* is very keen on tradition, heritage and 'never forgetting' all sorts of heroic British endeavours. Unfortunately, the great publishing institution appears to have accidentally forgotten one particularly heroic aspect of its own heritage – viz. their wholehearted support for the fascism of Hitler, Mussolini and Oswald Mosley. How terribly absent-minded of them.

Acclaim for Oswald Mosley's British Union of Fascists kicked off on 8 January 1934 with the unequivocal headline: 'Hurrah for the Blackshirts!' Some *Mail* staff even wore black shirts to work. Lord Rothermere, the paper's owner, wrote of the BUF in the 15 January 1934 issue that they were 'a well-organised party of the Right ready to take over responsibility for social affairs with the same directness of purpose and energy of method as Hitler and Mussolini displayed'. Oh, good.

Rothermere and the *Mail* broke with Mosley in June 1934, when the Blackshirts brutally suppressed (that is, kicked the shit out of) Communist Party supporters who disrupted a BUF meeting at the giant Olympia hall in Kensington, London – although not before investing (and now losing) £70,000 in New Epoch Products Ltd, a business arrangement with Mosley whereby the Blackshirts were to sell cigarettes made by Rothermere.

Towards Mussolini, meanwhile, the *Mail* was 'always friendly' (S. J. Taylor, *The Great Outsiders: Northcliffe, Rothermere and the* Daily Mail). In November 1926, Italy's fascist supremo dropped a hand-written line to G. Ward Price, the paper's Chief Correspondent, congratulating him on his appointment as a director: 'My Dear Price, I am glad you have become a Director of the *Daily Mail*, and I am sure that your very popular and widely circulated newspaper will continue to be a sincere friend of fascist Italy. With best wishes and greetings, Mussolini.' (On my photocopy of the letter there is a PS – 'How's the bunions? Up the Arsenal!' – although, to be fair, I did pencil that in myself.)

Through the 30s, the *Mail* was 'the only major British daily to take a consistently pro-Nazi line': it 'stuck out like a sore thumb' (Richard Griffiths, *Fellow Travellers of the Right: British Enthusiasts for Nazi Germany 1933–39*). Rothermere penned a July 1933 leader, 'Youth Triumphant', praising the Nazi regime for its 'accomplishments, both spiritual and material'. True, he admitted, there had been 'minor misdeeds of individual Nazis', but these would certainly be 'submerged by the immense benefits that the new regime is already bestowing on Germany'. So complimentary was the article, the Nazis used it for propaganda.

Rothermere eventually struck up a friendship with Hitler – or 'My dear Führer' as he invariably began his regular correspondences – and visited him numerous times. Rothermere and Ward Price were among only three or four foreigners invited to Hitler's first ever dinner party at his official Berlin residence. Rothermere, ever the gent, presented the Führer with some Ferrero Rocher. Probably.

In 1937, Ward Price – who 'was believed to be Rothermere's mouthpiece not only by the public but by Ward Price himself'

(Taylor) – published a chatty memoir about his great mates Hitler and Mussolini entitled *I Know These Dictators*. Last revised and reprinted in August 1938 – when fascism's dark intents were obvious to even the most ardent reactionary – the book called Mussolini 'a successful man of the world who is expert at his job and enjoys doing it' and spoke warmly of Hitler's 'human, pleasant personality'. The chapter 'The Human Side of Hitler' (not a phrase you hear very often) revealed that, alongside his affection for kiddies and doggies, the great dictator was also partial to the odd chocolate éclair: 'Naughty but nice', as the Führer used to say.

Price urged readers of *I Know These Dictators* to keep an 'open mind' on fascism. Of Hitler's initial wave of repression on gaining power, he wrote: 'The Germans were made to feel the firm hand of their new master. Being Germans, they liked it.'

The concentration camps – about which 'gross and reckless accusations [have been] made' – were just full of dirty Reds. The Night of the Long Knives, when Hitler took on his party rivals – by killing them all – was a sensible bit of forward planning avoiding the need for lots of silly arguments later on. Overall, 'in every respect of the German nation's life the constructive influence of the Nazi regime [was] seen'. The only people who suffered were a few troublesome 'minorities'. Like, for instance, the Jews.

In the chapter 'Germany's Jewish Problem' (the title's something of a giveaway), Price explains how the Jews only had themselves to blame as there had been too large a Jewish immigration to Germany following World War I: 'The cause of this migration was the collapse of the German currency, which gave the Jews of neighbouring countries a chance after their own heart to make big profits.'

Lord Rothermere last visited Hitler in May 1938. While other papers condemned the regime's brutality and oppression, the *Mail* still claimed Germany was 'in the forefront of nations' and that Hitler was 'stronger than ever and more popular with his countrymen'. On 1 October 1938, after the signing of the Munich treaty in which Britain and France appeased Germany's invasion of Czechoslovakia's disputed Sudetenland region, Rothermere sent a telegram to Hitler: 'MY DEAR FUHRER EVERYONE IN ENGLAND IS PROFOUNDLY MOVED BY THE BLOODLESS SOLUTION OF THE CZECHOSLOVAKIAN PROBLEM STOP PEOPLE NOT SO MUCH CONCERNED WITH TERRITORIAL READJUSTMENT AS WITH THE DREAD OF ANOTHER WAR WITH ITS ACCOMPANYING BLOODBATH STOP FREDERICK THE GREAT A GREAT POPULAR FIGURE IN ENGLAND MAY NOT ADOLF THE GREAT BECOME AN EQUALLY POPULAR FIGURE STOP I SALUTE YOUR EXCELLENCY'S STAR WHICH RISES HIGHER AND HIGHER.'

Oddly enough, 'Hitler the Great' never did become a popular figure in England or, indeed, any other part of the British Isles. When war was finally declared in September 1939, Rothermere reportedly uttered just two words: 'Ah' and then 'Bugger'.

Ward Price finally broke with Hitler following the March 1939 invasion of Czechoslovakia. Only a 'foreign policy issue' (Griffiths) could provoke this shift in his opinions: 'Germany's internal policies, even at the extreme moment of the Kristallnacht Pogrom, could never have had such an effect.'

Strangely, though, that's not how he remembered the whole thing afterwards. In his 1957 memoir, *Extra-Special Correspondent*, he 'recalls' how he always thought Hitler was weak and neurotic. Saw through it all from the start. Never even owned a black shirt. Some of his best friends, etc., etc.

Price was clearly suffering from an affliction still rife at the paper today: a version of false memory syndrome that makes you forget you used to be a bit of an old fascist.

It can only but make you wonder what would have happened if the Nazis had won the war. Presumably in the newly fascist Britain they would soon have found a collaborator in their old friend Rothermere. Then we might have ended up with a *Daily Mail* pouring forth reactionary bile against immigrants, gays, trade unionists, asylum seekers, women . . .

Dance music as The Future

In the 90s, many people thought dance music was The Future Of Music And The Future Of Everything, that catching a few DJ sets by Sister Bliss would eventually forge young people together as The Oneness – a single bubbling, bouncing organism strong enough to move any mountain. Although why you would want to move mountains is beyond me. Moving a mountain is the sort of project you would only embark upon if you were completely off your tits.

These days, dance music's main function is to introduce young people to such futuristic 'soundz' as Jefferson Airplane (Boogie Pimps), early 80s Stevie Winwood (Eric Prydz) and the Electric Light Orchestra (The Lovefreekz).

And that is the story of dance music.

Dead prostitutes

Why are all telly crime thrillers centred around dead prostitutes? Jesus, prostitution must be fairly tough already, without some hack bumping you off every ten minutes. I'm surprised there are any left. And it's not even enough for them to be 'dead'. Most of them also have to be 'mutilated'.

Prime Suspect alone, which begins with the identification of the brutally murdered corpse of prostitute Della Mornay, racked up six. And that's just the first series. *The Vice*? The name's a right giveaway: wall-to-wall dead tarts; they might as well put a counter in the corner of the screen marking the time until the first one goes toes up.

And it's not just on the telly. Glance at any crime/thriller book reviews and you'll find: 'Dr Tony Hill is a clinical psychologist whose assistance is often sought by DCI Carol Jordan, with whom he conducts a hesitant waltz of the "will they/won't they?" variety. The mutilated body of a prostitute has been found.' Has it? No shit.

Right next to this, in the *Guardian Review*, 31 July 2004, we find: 'Maverick American director Johnny Vos is in the city to make a film about the Belgian surrealist painter Paul Delvaux, but his female extras (recruited mainly from the red light district [check!]) start turning up dead [check!], their mutilated bodies [check!] accompanied by videos of Kumel's films.'

That Lynda La Plante alone gets through more ladies of the night than Wayne Rooney. If you're a prostitute and you see La Plante coming – and, let's face it, you're not going to fucking miss her, even in the dark – run for your life.

Not content with icing hookers, La Plante's very aura seems to bring danger to staff of her own production company. She told the *Observer*: 'The darkness is all around us. It's very easy to see. It's down there in the street. We just had a guy screaming abuse, stark naked, trying to knife somebody over there in broad daylight. We've had four rapes in this street. Every single girl in my office has been mugged and burgled – sometimes repeatedly. It is life.' Where is this office – in a crack house?

Alain de Botton
Whatever the subject, 'popular' 'intellectual' Alain de Botton will wade in with the most fatuously expected thing possible. Ask him about cooking duck and he'll say: 'Very fatty.' Ask him about Les Dawson's piano playing and he'll say: 'To play the piano that badly, he actually had to play the piano really well. I've read loads of Proust, you know.'

De Botton makes a handsome living from variations on a single phrase: 'Ah, but does it?' So, for the Art of Travel, he will say: 'Travel broadens the mind, they say. Ah, but does it?' And for On Love, he will say: 'Love makes us happy, they say. Ah, but does it?' Throw in a few banalities, raid philosophy and literature to reduce some of the greatest endeavours of human thought to a self-help soundbite, lunchy.

Sadly, as a small child Alain never grew any hair down the central dome of his head. This meant that he grew up with the nickname Alain 'Head As Smooth As A Baby's Bottom' de Botton. This is partly why he is so interested in the concept of status anxiety.

Ah, but is it?

Delicatessen counters at supermarkets
The pakoras piled up in that quaint earthenware bowl are, of course, produced by the Indian matriarch up to her elbows in ghee out the back, merrily crushing her own spices while

joshing with the French peasant dropping off filthy cheese in his 2CV.

Either that, or they've been mass-produced, loaded into plastic containers, transported across the country in a big lorry, removed from the plastic containers and placed into said earthenware bowl to seem just ever so slightly more appealing than the absolutely identical ones in vacuum-sealed plastic multipacks on the shelves.

Pasta salad? They've just cooked some pasta and then let it go cold.

I will not take a number. I am a free man.

Democrats, the

Clearly, some freaky voodoo madness is currently overtaking the States and, clearly, the Democrats are less evil than the Republicans – less bigoted, less likely to wage biblical wars for patently made-up reasons. But it's hard to see them as much of a port in any storm when, faced with this madness, they don't say: 'No more madness', but instead opt for: 'Well, okay then . . . some madness, if we must . . .'

And being 'less evil' than the Republicans doesn't actually equal being 'good'. Certainly, in terms of being a progressive force in US politics, the Democrats have come on since the days they were dominated by Southern slave owners – but they voted for Bush's civil liberties-busting Patriot Act, and the Iraq War, and are right up to their shitty necks in corporate funding.

For many years, John Kerry actually topped the Senate's business donations league, trousering a cool $1 million from the telecoms industry alone. Personally investing in the telecoms industry while also, coincidentally, sitting on the House's telecoms committee, Kerry has pushed through a host of legislation favourable to – you'll never guess – the telecoms industry. Given all this, it wasn't too hard for Republicans to portray him as a greasy-pole favour-monkey who doesn't really give a fuck. He is. And he doesn't.

Unsurprisingly, Kerry often struggled to mean anything whatsoever. Okay, he did recognise the war as a key issue. Sadly, it was the wrong war: the Vietnam War, which finished, ooh, ages ago. Lucky he didn't start banging on about Custer's Last Stand. A key Kerry slogan – of almost divine emptiness – proclaimed: 'Let America be America again.' Yes, let's put all this talk of America being Scandinavia behind us. It's America, can't you see? It's right there on the map! In big letters! Scandinavia's right over there . . .

Eventually, Kerry having exuded all the strained charm of an undertaker giving a father-of-the-bride speech, Clinton was wheeled out to add some much needed 'glamour'. These days, Clinton is seen as the last great 'progressive' US President, the 90s Good Guy who stands up for fine, admirable things like books. But Clinton's primary loyalties were always to the people dishing out the campaign dosh, like the auto and arms industries. And how progressive was his flagship pledge to 'end welfare as we know it' – which he did not by overhauling the meagre benefits system to favour the neediest, but instead by quite literally *ending* welfare, cancelling the benefits of pregnant women who didn't take low-paid jobs? About as progressive as someone cleaning the wax out of your ears with a soldering iron.

Clinton's New Democrats even invented a new political word, 'triangulation', to denote using progressive rhetoric to pacify voters while continuing to do the bidding of big business. But really, two old words would have sufficed: 'telling' and 'lies'.

For many Americans, the Democrats' appeal remains: you have no one else to vote for. When there is someone else to vote for, as when anti-corporate activist Ralph Nader stood in 2000 and 2004, the Democrats get so angry they can barely form sentences. In 2000, they blamed Nader for 'losing' them the election by taking their votes. Considering Nader stood on a completely different platform (welfare provision, environmentalism, jobs, etc.), this is like the Tories blaming the loss of a marginal on the turnout for the Socialist-Green Unity Coalition.

Here are some great slogans for the Democrats to use in the next presidential election:

'I did not have fiscal relations with that corporation.'

'Okay, I did.'

'Senator John Kerry, reporting for duty – where are my expenses?'

'Let Scandinavia be Spain again.'

'I was in a war, you know.'

'Read my lips: no new taxes.'

'Let Spain be Indonesia again.'

'Oh, go on, pleeaaaassse, we're a bit less shit than the other lot. What? No! You can't go off with them! But, but . . . you can't! You just can't! Waaah!'

Designer baby clothes

NEW DAD: Hey, here's an idea – let's get the baby a Daisy & Tom cardie for 50 quid that it'll probably grow out of tomorrow afternoon.

NEW MUM: Great. Do they do ickle baby socks in, like, gold thread? That'd be good.

NEW DAD: Yes, it's so important to dress the baby right – you know, to dangle wealth off it.

NEW MUM: Mmm. Otherwise, what's the point?

NEW DAD: Maybe we could get a head-to-toe outfit from Moschino? Is that what Tim and Candelabra got for little, erm, baby? Or was it DKNY?

NEW MUM: Tricky. What would Gwyneth do? Oh, and then there's I Pinco Pallino! They're Italian, so that's some educational value right there.

NEW DAD: And what about those £1000 Silver Cross prams? I WANT ONE!! I mean . . . the baby wants one.

NEW MUM: Fucking wicked, yeah!

NEW DAD: We could pimp it up real good – jack up the wheels, get some 26-inch tyres on those babies, some leopard skin goin' down . . . Cristal, pick up some bitches . . . ooh, yeah! I'm all excited . . . I think I'll put the Groove Armada CD on.

NEW MUM: Um, darling, you know what? I've been thinking . . . I'm actually quite bored of the baby now – I mean, we've had it for, like, eight weeks or something. Maybe we could drop him off at a charity shop or something? Like with shoes.

Diddy Day

Anyone still wondering whether America's moral code has gone through some particularly rusty scrambler should consider that Las Vegas has now instituted 14 May as Diddy

Day – a special day to commemorate that latter-day Martin Luther King, P Diddy. 'Our hope is that he continues to bring his electrifying presence to Las Vegas,' said Mayor Oscar Goodman.

What he might have done instead was to declare 14 May as Dido Diddy Diddy Dodo Day – a special day dedicated to the female singer-songwriter, the 'electrifying' urban music mogul and the extinct flightless bird formerly native to Mauritius.

I'm not saying that would have been better, but it would have been different.

A bugger to organise, though.

Disaster relief porkies

When it comes to disasters, Western governments are like pissed uncles: forever making wild promises they have no intention of keeping.

When Hurricane Mitch devastated Central America in 1998, £4.8 billion was pledged by governments, but only £1.6 billion of it, or 33%, was ever delivered. After floods struck Mozambique in 2000, £214 million was pledged by governments – but only £107 million, or 50%, was delivered.

Most startling is the fact that, of the $1.1 billion pledged after the Bam earthquake in Iran in 2003, only $17 million ever turned up. That's 2%. That's one seriously pissed uncle talking some serious pissed shit about taking you to the zoo and stuff.

'We never get all the money we are pledged,' says Elizabeth Byrs of the UN's Office for the Co-ordination of Humanitarian Affairs. As well as simply not paying up, governments also pull neat accounting tricks like diverting money that was to go to other needy situations, or making a big fuss of suspending affected countries' debt repayments but all the while allowing the interest to mount up, so when the country does start repaying it has a whacking great sum to pay back.

Harry Edwards, a spokesperson for USAID, the US government agency responsible for distributing humanitarian and economic assistance funds, said: 'A lot of countries don't pay. The United States isn't the only one.'

He later claimed that, anyway, a bigger boy had made him do it.

Another trick is to count money spent on the military who may offer assistance as part of the total – that is, use the disaster as a way of subsidising the military, recouping military expenditure from your supposed charitable donation. Is there nothing the US will not milk to fund the military? I'm surprised there aren't neo-cons wandering round the White House looking for stuff to melt down: 'This big stampy thing and the pad – the one with the eagle on it – do we actually need this? We do? Okay. What about this picture of Abraham Lincoln? No one remembers who the fuck he was anyway, let's put it on eBay.'

Il Divo

Italian for 'The Divs'.

Doctors

In June 2005, a *Real Story* documentary offered a compelling reason why so many GPs manage that trademark double whammy of talking in slow, patronising tones while also being utterly hopeless in the actual 'helping people' department: they are either pissed up or high on drugs.

Or rather, one in 15 of them is, anyway. The others are just gits.

Incidentally, Fiona Bruce trailed the programme with the line: 'Your life in their boozy hands.'

Doctors on daytime TV

There's something that doesn't really scream Hippocratic ideals about being paid cartloads of cash for sitting around on a sofa chatting about hysterectomies.

Also, they're always so fucking nice to everyone, which makes me think they can't possibly be real doctors.

'Doctors' on daytime TV, as in the programme called *Doctors*, the one that's on before *Murder, She Wrote* . . .

. . . with the intro sequence featuring the words 'doctors doctors doctors doctors doctors doctors' flying across the screen – just in case you were in doubt about the profession the programme called *Doctors* might be centring on. That the standard of this daytime soap is barely a step up from the standard corporate safety film about wearing goggles raises the question: will nobody think of the old people and the students?

Dough balls

Executive version of overpriced toast. (See **Toast, overpriced**.)

Downsizers

Jennifer Lopez recently told *Cosmopolitan* she was jumping aboard the downsizing bandwagon. 'You get to a point where you want to strip down,' the singer-actress explained. 'I'm going to sell that big museum-type house and get a nice cosy house, and I'm going to have one car and trade the others in. I want to go back to something simpler.'

It doesn't matter how many rocks that she's got, she's just Jenny the former marketing executive from Islington moving to a croft on Stornoway.

Clearly, there are many ways of being less tosserish in life. But, surely, one of those ways involves not farting on and on about how much your standard of living has improved since you 'cut out all the crap and left all that mess behind'. It's no big deal – you are, after all, probably just living around people who never upsized in the first place; in the process, pushing up the property prices to the point that they too have to 'downsize', to a tent.

These burnt-out escapees could even develop some vague self-awareness that, with their 'opting out of the system' one-upmanship, they are actually another kind of 'cutting-edge taste-maker', colonising outposts and alerting marketing departments to profit possibilities.

Remember that last little trip to Starbucks you made before you left for mid-Wales? They put a microchip in your neck and are monitoring your movements, planning to use the data to locate new store-opening opportunities. They do the same thing to those Thai travellers who only carry one sock at a time and call everyone else 'tourists'.

Incidentally, Downsizer.net offers sound advice on how to survive without a delicatessen nearby. 'Try foraging for your food,' it suggests. 'The hedgerows, fields and woods have a surprising amount to offer'. Doesn't the countryside have enough problems without burnt-out stockbrokers digging around for grubs?

Dustmen refusing to fund free education

One of New Labour's key arguments used for crapping student grants out of the window and introducing top-up fees was: 'Why should the dustman of today pay for the lawyer of tomorrow?'

With the average student debt now running at £18,000, perhaps it's time to revisit that argument to see if, on closer inspection, the dustmen really could be contributing a bit more here. Because, you know, they're shirking their responsibilities on this one a bit, and that is not the New Britain way.

Among the money-raising ideas dustmen might take up are:

- Putting a big jar in the staff room that everyone can pitch their coppers into.
- Sponsored walks.
- Cleaning up stuff out of the bins and selling it at a booty.
- Taxing the rich. No, NOT taxing the rich. That is stupid. DO NOT try to tax the rich. Not now. Not ever.

DVDs with adverts you can't skip

The target group for these ads is quite small – the sort of person who wants to watch the same clip from *Only Fucking Fools and Bastard Horses* EVERY SINGLE TIME THEY USE THEIR DVD. Because the BBC has ensured that the option of skipping the advert reel and going straight to the menu has been disabled. Ho, ho, ho, there's Ricky Gervais doing that funny dance. Again.

The other thing DVD production bastards do is stop you skipping the copyright information – and then put it in 782 different languages, with a running time of seven hours. Just in case you thought it was perfectly legal to burn copies of DVDs but only if you went to Norway and did it.

Non-skippable adverts are like ITV modifying your telly so that if you press the mute button during the ads and try to get up to put the kettle on, you get a huge surge of electricity through your sex parts. And even ITV haven't sunk that low yet.

E

Early in/late home

Wrong way round. Surely?

Eats, Shoots and Leaves

If you're going to write a snooty book about punctuation and grammar, at least punctuate the title correctly. Honestly.

Election planes

Just when you thought politicians couldn't get more remote and less connected to actual people, they go aeronautical. The 2005 election was the first to see the leaders of the major parties using planes to get about; and you can't get much more remote than being actually up in the sky.

Blair, Howard, Kennedy – they were all up there being served tiny packets of pretzels, watching *Shrek II* with headphones on. At one point, Blair's plane was even hit by lightning. As a religious man, you'd think he'd take this as a sign. But he didn't. According to BBC Radio Five Live presenter Peter Allen, he was 'imperturbable' (that means 'he didn't shit himself').

In an hilarious mix-up, the Lib Dems accidentally got taken up in an RAF bomber. It was more or less clear that they hadn't wanted to campaign in this manner ideally, but once the bomber was up, how could they possibly question it? As it was, Charles Kennedy got so into it he said of the campaign, 'This really is moving from the ground war to the air war', conjuring up images of him sitting up there in a tin hit, smoking fags.

Sadly for Respect, the new party seeking to put religion at the forefront of politics, the contacts that might have lent George Galloway an Iraqi fighter jet have moved on. But if he seeks funds from other sympathetic regimes, like the Saudis and the remaining Stalinist states, the MP for Ba'athnal and Bow should be airborne next time. Indefatigably.

The Greens were having none of it, though. They scoffed at the planes and launched their manifesto on bicycles – old bicycles too, bought second-hand or found in canals. Which only shows why they will never break into the mainstream: if you can't see the importance of flying two hours to a remote airfield in Scotland to shake hands for 10 minutes with some carefully chosen party workers bussed in from Birmingham before reboarding for London again, you are simply not fit to lead this great country of ours.

No, what the British public wants – and what it is the democratic right of the British public to have – are meticulously orchestrated press stunts: they want a shot on the TV news of the Prime Minister delivering two sentences in front of a campaign poster that could have been done in a studio but was actually shot in Arbroath because it looks more 'genuine'.

Personally, I was sad to see papers announcing the death knell of the battle bus. Only John Prescott still operated in the old style; he remained 'under the radar', nomadically traversing the highways to hit, as the official strategy papers put it, 'anywhere that the press is not'.

Prescott fucking loved it: sausages for breakfast and his own PlayStation. There were apparently some issues with him mooning out of the window and getting wedged in the chemical toilet, but otherwise it was a largely incident-free trip. He didn't even hit anyone, although he did take to task some bastard journalist in South Wales who had the temerity to ask him some questions. 'Bugger off!' he said. Now *that's* campaigning.

The new plane strategy was a massive success for Labour: they were elected on the lowest ever mandate for a government. But, more importantly, no real people managed to say the word 'hospital' within 20 yards of Blair.

And that's what Great British democracy is all about.

E-mail bragging

People who 'complain' about how many messages they get sent, especially after they get back from holiday – 'I'm still ploughing through them!' Yes, well done. You're really fucking important.

Tracey Emin

In 2004, the Tate picked, of all the Sensation-al Young British Artists to preserve for 'The Nation', Tracey Emin, awarding her a room (to display work in, not to live in) at Tate Britain, where they keep the proper olden-days paintings.

This is fair enough, because Tracey Emin is as important an artist as Picasso. This is the view of at least some authorities on modern art. Such as Tracey Emin. She told Sue Lawley on *Desert Island Discs*: 'As an artist, to get some kind of notoriety or some kind of credit or fame, then you have to make a seminal piece of work, or you have to change the face of what people understand as art . . . I've done that with two pieces . . . I've done it with my tent and I've done it with my bed. Picasso did it with cubism.' Of course.

Perhaps Tate boss Nick Serota is simply trying to make the Tate accessible. Beds, bits of sewing, a feature film, a forthcoming book *all* tackle one fairly simple theme: how Emin had a bad time as a teenager in Margate and thus feels pain. This couldn't be more the case even if she just wrote 'I had a bad time as a teenager in Margate and thus feel pain' on a piece of paper and exhibited it. Which she probably has done.

But what next? Now that Tracey Emin is in the pantheon of treasured British artists, is there anywhere left for her to go? Is there anything she has not yet done to express her pain? When *i-D* magazine asked her if 'there [is] anything that's too painful or personal to become art', Emin said: 'Yes, of course. I had to have a camera up my bottom and, afterwards, the hospital insisted on giving me the film because I am an artist, but I passed out just looking at the screen. It wasn't that I hadn't had anything up my arse before, but I doubt whether I'd ever use the film in my art.'

So visitors to Tate Britain should rest assured they will only see the metaphorical, and not the literal, inside of Tracey Emin's arse. And for that, at least, may 'The Nation' be truly thankful.

Equality of opportunity

'A society. Where everyone. Or at least. Those who are. Very good. Boys and girls. Can rise up. On their own merit. And be free. Of the shame. And the guilt. Of being working class. No limits. No no. There's no limits. This beat is technocratic. Pump up the jam. And so on.'

'Equality of opportunity' is a cunning political phrase beloved of New Labour because it includes the word 'equality' – which has been fairly popular with Labour supporters over the years and means ending rank and privilege, nurturing everyone in society, sharing out the booty fairly equitably, that kind of thing – while meaning something completely different: 'Equality? What, for the poor? Fuck off. They shall have to get busy with their boot straps, I've a consultancy for a private healthcare company to attend to.'

The term 'meritocracy' (now used to denote a society where all receive a fair chance to get ahead and where everyone finds their 'right station' in life according to their own individual merits, not to their background) was invented by Michael Young (Toby Young's father, of all things) in a 1958 novelistic satire. *The Rise of the Meritocracy* portrayed a world controlled by smug, self-righteous bastards who thought they were always right because they were the best and where poor underachievers were at the bottom purely because of their own personal failings.

Young understood that, in such a society, it would not necessarily be the 'best' who came out on top, just those who are most enthusiastic about standing on the faces of everyone else.

And he hadn't even met Alan Milburn.

Estate agents showing people around houses on telly

ESTATE AGENT: So, here's the bathroom.

PERSON ON THE TELLY: Okay . . .

ESTATE AGENT: And, uh, the second bedroom – quite a nice size . . .

PERSON ON THE TELLY: Mmm.

It's amazing how often you can see estate agents showing people around houses on telly.

Ethical consumer scams

Spotting liberal soft touches from a distance of 40 miles, supermarkets have been known to mark up Fairtrade goods to make them more profitable than non-Fairtrade items. So the small coffee producer is getting slightly more for his goods. The conscience-driven consumer, on the other hand, is getting fleeced to fuckery. This is 'ethical', apparently.

Even if you don't buy your Cafédirect in a supermarket, world capitalism is not exactly quaking in its Jimmy Choo boots. Clearly a few small producers getting more for their coffee beans is not a bad thing, but Fairtrade accounts for only 0.001% of world trade. Even in areas where Fairtrade is strongest, their market share is puny: 3% of the UK coffee market and 4% of the banana market.

Meaning that, as a strategy for changing the world and challenging the structures of global power, 'buying coffee' is possibly not the most effective.

So . . . thank fuck we've got those wristbands as well.

Exciting developments in advertising

In 2004, Baz 'Moulin Rouge' Luhrmann made a five-minute, $12-million advert for Chanel No. 5 starring Nicole Kidman. Except he didn't – because, according to some quite major authorities such as Luhrmann's publicist, it was not an advert but a 'film'. This 'creative first' was, he said, 'the film to revolutionise advertising'.

Many others commented on how this 'film' radically broke down the barriers between commerce and art – which it did. It broke down the barriers between commerce and art by the commerce side kicking the barriers to pieces then lumping the art side with a tyre iron.

Meanwhile, plans are afoot in the US for interactive technology to let viewers instantly purchase products they see being used by TV/movie characters in product placements. Just to be absolutely clear about this, Baz: that's a bad thing.

Exercise videos

Here is a fun quiz. Which is the weirdest exercise video of them all? Is it:

- *Ultimate Results with Beverly Callard*. aka Liz McDonald from *Corrie*. This is THE video for all those people whose 'ultimate result' is looking like a startled ginger giraffe.
- *Anna Kournikova's Basic Elements*. Combines a workout with an elementary chemistry lesson.
- *Patsy Palmer's Ibiza Workout*. Which shows you how to get fit by necking lots of Ecstasy tablets and contracting an STD. Possibly.

- *Davina McCall's The Power of 3*. How to get fit while using a video mobile.
- *Daniella Westbrook's Better Body*. Includes those all-important nose exercises.
- *Lynne Robinson's Pilates with Fern Britton*. Now, I don't in any way want to denigrate someone for their physical appearance, but I'm saying if you're marketing a range of exercise videos, Fern Britton is not really the image you want to project. If you were marketing a range of biscuits, maybe.
- *Tantra t'ai Chi Fitness (Adult Educational)*. Eh? Eh? I'll say.
- *Kate Lawler's 'Kate's Cardio Combat'*. In which the *Big Brother* winner takes on the seemingly unbeatable Russian monster Drago to avenge the death of her friend Apollo Creed. Actually, no, now I come to think about it, that's *Rocky IV*.

Exposé documentaries which are not

In recent years, Channel 5 has left behind all that wispy-drapes rumpo to become a proper TV channel, fulfilling an urgent public service brief to keep the public informed on today's vital issues: mummies, dictators and how to fly a Spitfire.

Sometimes, though, they let their rigorous standards slip and put out hack pieces with no new facts or footage but with a sexed-up title and risqué trailer promising to blow the lid off all sorts of dark and sultry secrets.

Secrets of the Beatles promised to expose years of Fab Four secrecy – the build-up looked like it was going to tell how they were all secret lovers in league with the Devil. In the event, the programme revealed that the group was 'very popular in the 1960s' and that 'Ringo' was a fake name. *The Real Richard and Judy*? They really are called Richard and Judy. And they really are married.

This is unsatisfactory all round. If you really want to sex it up to get the punters in, why not just completely make the documentaries up? Here's a few to get you started:

- Full Egyptian Sex.
- Mummified D-Day Shag Bandits.
- Hitler, Mummified, At It – In Colour.
- When Jordan Met Von Ribbentrop.
- I'm A Nude Dunkirk Tommy – Get Me Out Of Here!

F

Faith schools

At 1996's pre-victory Labour conference, Tony Blair declared that in power he would prioritise three things: 'Education, education and education.' What he should have said was: 'I'm one serious Christian right here.'

God helps you learn stuff. Everyone knows this. If God's there glaring over your shoulder, it really focuses the mind on understanding how glaciation works. No one can put the fear of God into you like God. Don't think He can't see you drawing a penis on to Henry VIII's forehead in that textbook. He's a big bugger too, so watch out.

In 21st century Britain – a place where people think more about John Leslie than about God – a quarter of all schools are now allied to a faith. The nation is blessed with Anglican schools, Catholic schools, Muslim schools, Sikh schools, evangelical schools, Seventh-Day Adventist schools; in Hereford there are even plans for a school that worships Thor, the Norse God of Thunder, where pupils can specialise in bolt-throwing, beard maintenance, warmongering and, of course, thunder.

In Parliament, Tony Blair even defended one school's right to teach Creationism alongside evolution, claiming that 'a more diverse school system will deliver better results'. In a sense, this is correct. Creationism and Darwinism are both simply theories on how the human race came into being. But where Darwinism is a theory that allies itself with logic, Creationism is a theory that allies itself with making stuff up and pretending it's true.

In C of E schools around Canterbury, teachers have been instructed on how to induce a state of hypnotism – or 'guided meditation' – in five-year-old children by lighting candles, closing curtains and asking them to close their eyes before lullingly evoking images of the Last Supper.

The teacher tells the children to imagine an old-fashioned room with a big bowl of 'delicious-smelling stew'. They are carrying this receptacle into another room where long-robed men are gathering. As everyone sits down, the children must envisage Jesus entering through the front door and ask them-selves: 'What does he look like? . . . Is he clean-shaven or bearded? . . . Happy or sad? . . . Everybody greets him, includ-ing you . . . Jesus takes the bread that you set out and breaks it in half and says: "Take this and eat, because this is my body" . . . How does he look? . . . The bread comes along and everybody breaks off a piece and eats it . . . What does it taste like?'

Erm, like bread? The diocesan schools adviser does admit this process can 'produce deep emotions'. You can say that again – I've just lost my fucking lunch.

Britain's most worrying new educationalist is evangelical second-hand car magnate Sir Peter Vardy. At his flagship Emmanuel College in Gateshead, pupils have to carry not one but two Bibles, which, even if you're quite big on the whole Bible thing, does seem excessive.

So how does God influence the teaching? This was spelt out in a controversial document – now removed from their web-site – called 'Christianity and the Curriculum', which reckons science classes should show how 'the study of science is not an end in itself but a glimpse into the rational and powerful hand of the Almighty'. Art classes should show how art can 'serve the glory of God and celebrate the complex beauty of His creation'. At which point, even the Scouse bloke who does *Art Attack* on CBBC starts feeling his intelligence being insulted.

The document went on to say – and this is genuinely not made up – that History lessons could usefully consider whether, during World War II, Britain was saved from Hitler by God intervening to halt the Nazis at the Channel. Meaning that maybe the Battle of Britain film classic *Reach For The Skies* could more accurately have been called *Reach From The Skies With A Big Fuck-Off Finger Saying, NOT SO FAST, MR HITLER!*

I personally think it's a crying shame that no school in the land teaches my own theory of creation: that this whole grand enterprise is merely an imaginative figment of my Uncle Mick who smokes a pipe and seems to live entirely on toasted sandwiches. I firmly believe that he dreamed the whole thing up one afternoon while watching the Channel 4 racing, which he loves, and the moment he gets bored, that's it, we're all toast, just like one of Uncle Mick's delicious sandwiches.

I was going to set a school up, but I couldn't be bothered.

Fascist teachers

Far be it from me to take up the baton for 'standards' in education, but I can't be the only person taken aback by teachers being members of the BNP. Maybe they lowered the entry qualifications for teacher training and I hadn't noticed: 'What's that, mate – your own Blockbusters membership? Come on in . . .'

In 2004, Solihull maths teacher Simon Smith was finally

suspended only after declaring his intention to stand for the thickie far-right outfit in the Euro elections (whether his Amazing Dancing Bear is also a right fascist wasn't made clear). Smith's personal website had links to other far-right groups, 'revisionist' historian David Irving, Hitler's *Mein Kampf* and eugenics websites. The site also outlined his thoughts on the Holocaust: 'The "six million" and "gas chambers" story is a lie.' So, almost definitely a fascist, then.

Smith went on to stand as a BNP candidate in the last general election. On local radio, he explained that blacks and Asians born in the UK could not be British because 'a dog born in a stable doesn't make it a horse'. Ah, but would the dog be British?

The BNP provided more evidence of possessing weapons grade idiocy in December 2004 when it booked a black DJ for a Christmas party. Croydon-branch organiser Bob Garner explained: 'He sounded white on the phone.'

Naturally, a number of guests at the £12-a-head event at a central London hotel walked out in disgust. However, 'some younger members thought it was a bit ironic and danced the night away'.

Okay, so do fascists dance ironically in the same way that annoying people dance ironically at works' Christmas parties? Or do they employ more discipline and menace?

Fashion journalism
Words to go with pictures of people wearing clothes written by boarding-school girls with misspelt first names (so many 'z's) and double-barrelled second ones.

At heart, fashion journalism isn't about clothes; it's about being so Now that by the time you've finished typing the word Now it's too late, because by now you're Then.

Among fashion journalism's key linguistic traits are:

- Sentences that resemble complicated Google searches: 'the Kate Moss/Jade Jagger/Sienna Miller school of Primrose Hill bling-meets-boho laid-back high-chic'. Keep up, ugly losers.
- Casually dropped French terminology – *'au courant'*, *'de la saison'* – in the style of popular sitcom character Delboy Trotter.
- Weird boasts. Like 'I'm a fashion innovator', 'I take classic Armani pieces and wear them in a modern way', 'I'm an accessories freak'. These are good things, presumably?
- Hyperbole. 'Oh Jesus, bite me on the arse these bags of the season are making me so high, they must be a gift from God!'
- Referring to people you have never met by their first names: Kate, Mario, Lemmy.
- Deification of models. Not just models modelling, but interviews with models about modelling too! Here's Karolina Kurkova, a model, on what it's like to be a model: 'It's not just about being cute. It's about creating something through light and clothes and expressions. It's like theatre.' This woman was the highest paid model in 2003, but we should feel very sorry for her: 'Modelling looks glamorous from the outside, but sometimes I have moments when I cry.' Yes, me too.

Sometimes fashion journalists get paid to write novels, like Plum Sykes's excruciating *Bergdorf Blondes*, a book which has apparently become 'a Bible for the fabulously wealthy, the inner circle elite'. And which proves, decisively, that you should never read books by anyone named after a fruit.

Fast-food chains marketing themselves as 'healthy' (and feminist)

'Hi – we're McDonald's, a great big company that would love to come round to your house and tell you about how we're changing.'

In the 1950s, French artist Yves Klein invented his own colour, International Klein Blue, which he believed represented *Le Vide* (the void) – not a vacuum or terrifying darkness, but a void that invokes positive sensations of openness and liberty, a feeling of profound fulfilment beyond the everyday and material. Standing before Klein's huge canvases of solid blue, many report being enveloped by serene, trance-like feelings.

I feel something very similar looking at the pictures of salads in the window of Kentucky Fried Chicken. Or that surreal meal deal with the plastic bowl of rice. You wouldn't actually order these items, but their very existence expresses that corporation's painful identity crisis faced with a shrinking market. Mmmm. Lovely.

I get similar buoyant sensations by reading the McDonald's Corporation's 2004 pamphlet '(We thought we'd come to you for a) Change', posted through letterboxes across the land, which bravely reconfigures McDonald's as a health-food restaurant and general harbinger of world peace. The tone of a spurned lover who treated you wrong and now sees the error of his ways pervades the whole document: 'Hi – we're McDonald's', it begins, 'a great big company that would love to come round to your house and tell you about how we're changing. But there are a lot of us and it takes ages to get organised.' That's a joke (no, really) to show us they have a Good Sense Of Humour.

'We've knocked the booze on the head and got a job. We've moved out of our mum's and got a flat: it's not much, but it's a home. It could be *our* home.' I made that last bit up.

The pamphlet desperately bids to woo everyone back to their formerly favourite restaurant: there are pictures of cute black children, pictures of cute moo cows, parents lovingly clasping their children's hands and a cute child on a swing – all brimming with salad-derived vitamins. In keeping with the identity crisis theme, there's also a picture of some paunchy blokes watching the football in a pub to reassuringly convey the message: yes, we do still sell shitty burgers that chew your guts up something rotten.

Another section, which contains some of the most remark-able prose ever written, aims to reposition McDonald's at the head of the feminist market (this is not made up). Headlined 'You go girls', the empowering passage claims that 'spending time away from the boys is a rare and precious thing. Make the most of it while you can. Take a shopping break, put the bags down and find somewhere fun to eat.' Because, this says, being a carer to men and shopaholic (which, of course, is the very essence of womanhood) is hard work. But where could you possibly have this break? 'Yoohoo! – we're over here.' Ah yes, McDonald's.

The text – and if you don't believe this actually happened, you can check it out: I've donated my copy to the British

Library – ends like this: 'Girls, before you know it, you'll be back home and showing the things you bought to the boys, and unless it's got cars or footballers on it – they won't care. So have a great day, have a great salad, and sisters? Do it for yourselves.'

Faux swearing

Strolling past The Shop Formerly Known As French Connection, have you ever been driven to splutter, giggle, tap your companion's shoulder and exclaim, 'Look, look – it almost says FUCK!'? I rather think you haven't.

Similarly, when you hear a panel show called *Stupid Punts*, there is unlikely to be a mass gasp of shock and exhilaration. Maybe some old people would be shocked – but they're unlikely to be watching BBC3. (Actually, most people are unlikely to be watching BBC3, but you take my point.) During the fox-hunting debate, there wasn't a news source in the land that could resist a cheeky play on the word 'fox'. The silly fucks.

There is nothing big or clever about pretending to swear. If you want to be big and clever you need to call your shop Spunky Fucking Tit-Monkey's Arsing Cockarama and Co. Now *that's* swearing.

Fax charges

In the Easiest Living Ever stakes, charging people for sending faxes is narrowly pipped into second place behind being the Duke of Westminster, who has topped the poll every year since 1951 when he was born owning half of London.

At a quid for the first sheet, followed by 50p for each subsequent sheet, a six-page fax sets you back £3.50. With the phone call to send the fax costing about 5p, that's a mark-up of 7000%.

Your local copy shop or 'fax bureau' Nazi would say that it's not just the cost of the call; they also need the 'infrastructure' – that 'infrastructure' being a very shit fax machine purchased in 1987. Ah yes, that explains it. Cheers.

Hugh Fearnley-Whittingstall

The whole River Cottage 'experiment' was just amazing. Surviving for a whole year only on what he can grow from the soil or barter. With nothing to fall back on but the enormous royalties from a best-selling book and hit TV series. Amazing.

According to a bloke I met in a pub, what people don't know about Fearnley-Whittingstall is that to facilitate the manoeuvres of the TV crew he had a three-lane motorway put in leading right up to River Cottage, totalling a vast expanse of natural beauty and causing the extinction of some species. And, following his trips there to get crabs and stuff, West Bay has now become so popular that Starbucks and McDonald's are planning to open branches there and British Nuclear Fuels are going to dump toxic waste in the water. This bloke had been drinking heavily, but still . . .

Incidentally, I'm surely not the only person to feel rather perturbed whenever I come across the phrase 'Hugh Fearnley-Whittingstall's Meat'? I'm coughing and spluttering in shock even before I've noticed this meat-based cookbook's price tag: £25.

In his romantic willingness to embrace the extremes of Nature, Hugh is turning into a Kurtz-like figure whose questing spirit puts him beyond the limits of human society. If he doesn't start reintegrating soon, there might be no hope of a safe return. Reconnaissance crews will be sent down the M3 to Dorset to find him dressed in cowhide and taking daily baths in goose fat.

£25? Think of all the meat you could buy with that. You could have it hanging around the house like Christmas decorations.

Otis Ferry

Otis thinks we don't understand his country ways. Maybe his dad should have visited the countryside in his full Roxy Music pomp – as an Elvis-matador-gayboy-from-Venus dragging behind him what looks like three welders in purple lippy – to see how much understanding he got. It could have saved everyone a lot of bother.

Otis Ferry is presumably called Otis after Otis Redding. Ha ha. Ha ha ha ha ha ha ha. Ha. The point I'm trying to make here is: YOU'RE HAVING A FUCKING LAUGH.

50 Cent

In April 2005, Reebok launched a TV ad campaign showing 50 Cent sat on a box in a burnt-out warehouse, snarling at the camera and counting to nine while the screen turns slowly red and a crackly newscaster reminds how 'he's been shot nine times'. Oddly, some thought the ad made getting shot look cooler than it often turns out to be.

It's certainly not his clever rhyme skills, so the fact that 50 Cent is now among the world's biggest entertainment figures apparently derives almost entirely from having got himself shot up nine whole times – something he doesn't like to talk about. Oh no, sorry. I was getting mixed up with the singer from Athlete. 50 Cent loves talking about shooting and getting shot up; he's regularly pictured wearing body armour, pointing massive shooters at the camera lens wearing an expression saying 'I'm gonna shoot you up'. He called his last album *The Massacre*, always starting beefs with other rappers about who is best at shooting and getting shot up. And so on.

All his bullet wounds were actually attained in one incident, but his image rather portrays someone who has trouble visiting the local shop without getting himself shot up: 'Honey! I got shot up again . . . Ooooweee, this one's a biter . . . got any bandaids left or did we run out after last week? Oo!'

Reebok responded to the complaints by claiming the 50 Cent ad campaign was a 'positive and empowering celebration of his right of freedom of self-expression'. And not his 'right of freedom' to get shot right up.

Film stars

Hollywood film stars on chat shows: you have to ask – would you let them near small children?

Here's Tom Cruise: laughing much too hard, slapping his thighs and hooting at stuff that's not particularly funny. Who actually slaps their thighs when they hear something funny? Blimey, now he's rocking backwards and forwards . . .

Oh, and here's Kevin Spacey: talking and moving as though he's been glazed, clearly having given the producers the brief that he will only appear as long as he can try and kill the audience to death by boring on about Bobby Darin instead of tackling any amusing issues about his intriguing private life and demanding pets.

Oh fuck, here comes Meg Ryan for her bravura perform-ance on *Parkinson*: actually, Meg's decision to appear on a chat show and not chat was at least fairly radical. She did depart from the whole everyone's-loving-each-other's-company form and became utterly despised in the process. So well done, Meg. You big freak.

Film warnings

What's a childhood without a few sleepless nights spent haunted by the memory of a grim celluloid bloodbath? Kids love it. Waking up in the middle of the night, sweating, fever-ishly recalling a zombie axeman hacking at some poor unfortunate's innards? That's the magic of childhood, that is. Sadly, however, some people don't see it that way and want to deny any potential for trauma with film warnings that seem to get more convoluted by the month.

But really, what kind of person would want to stop anyone seeing a film that 'contains mild peril'? There are, according to some estimates, only seven basic storylines in all human art, all of which contain at least some peril. It's what makes them stories. And even 'mild peril' sounds fairly pathetic; like 'mild action violence' or 'mild sensuality'. If a film is going to include peril, action violence and sensuality – and, clearly, it should – then ideally the usage should not be mild. At the very least, it should be 'moderate'.

Who demanded such stultifying detail? There surely don't

exist people who read the cinema listings and think, 'Oh dear, no. We can't go and see the new Spiderman film, it's got one use of strong language and mild sensuality – if little Daisy sees that, she might die.' Or is this, perhaps, America's family-centric right extending its icy influence over the listings in your local free paper? Hell's teeth, it's even got 'thematic elements'!

To be truly sensitive to a young person's individual fears, we should probably detail everything that may cause offence: 'One scene takes place in a kitchen, which features a major heat source ... plus there is one use of a staircase – down which someone might potentially fall. Also involves moderate use of hair and teeth.'

Fish symbols on cars

Early Christians used a fish symbol to identify fellow believers during times of persecution. These days, to let people know they are really into Jesus, many Christians stick a fish sign on the back of their car. Like Baby On Board stickers – but with God-knobs on.

In the US, these symbols have caused belief-system-related mayhem. This is because the symbols don't just mean 'I'm the nice sort of Christian who sometimes distributes hot soup to the homeless', but are more likely to mean: 'Science is witchcraft and you're all going to hell.' To underline the hard-right/anti-science/anti-abortion intent, some fish contain the word 'Bush' inside indicating that George W. is 'doing God's work'.

Incensed, humanists created their own bumper fish symbols with the word 'Darwin' inside hoping to irritate the

Christian right. It worked. They didn't like it. It got nasty. Chris Gilman, the Hollywood special-effects whizz who apparently invented the Darwin fish, said: 'Here's a religion about forgiveness, peace, and love, but I can't tell you how many times I've heard about Darwin fish being torn off of cars and broken.'

The Christians retaliated with a bumper sticker depicting the Darwin fish being swallowed by a larger 'Jesus', or 'Truth', fish.

The humanists shot back with a reversed version of the sticker.

Then the Ring of Fire website produced a sticker depicting the Darwin fish and the Jesus fish forming 'what Shakespeare jauntily termed the beast with two backs' (they were at it, like knives).

Nothing will wind up a right-wing Christian more than piscine penetration faith denigration. And so it proved, with yet more car park/highway altercations.

Actually, this is possibly a good way finally to settle the evolution/creation debate: a demolition derby on the highway with the loser ending up bleeding in a ditch with bits of car stuck in them.

If the Christians won, they could shout back at the twisted wreckage: 'What's that you said about survival of the fittest? I CAN'T HEAR YOU!!!'

Food advice

There is some useful food advice: 'Eat Your Fucking Greens Or You Will Die.'

But for many this is simply not self-absorbed enough so

they send cash to strange nutritionists in exchange for magic beans and kelp.

The main problems with the nutritional advice of 'food experts' are that:

1. Even supposedly sound advice reverses every two months. Don't go to work on an egg any more; an egg a day will make your arteries swell up like hose pipes (hose pipes full of cancer). Fish? Well, of course. Oh, but maybe not fish that's been pulled from our polluted seas. Or fish that was reared on a fish farm. Oh hell.

2. They turn healthy eating into the kind of task that would make Hercules say: 'Bollocks to that for a game of soldiers.' Fruit for breakfast is great – but not oranges or orange juice. Orange juice is bad for breakfast! You might as well just eat cancer. If you opt for grapes, don't mix them with anything else. And don't eat spinach unaccompanied by vitamin C or your body won't absorb the goodness. Getting the body to absorb 'the goodness' is petrifyingly difficult: we're all living on a knife edge here.

3. Many nutritional 'doctors' received their Ph.D.s from the Quacky-Duck University, Land of Make-Believe, and so are about as real doctors as Dr Dre or Dr Fox. Dr Fox isn't even a real fox.

4. Because many people have already heard about broccoli and tomatoes, the experts justify their existence by recommending alternative foodstuffs that don't resemble food. Even if you wanted to, you can't buy these items – 'ayurvedic cleansing tri herb combination Triphala' – anywhere in the

world except on their personal websites. Even seemingly rational books recommend 'incorporating paprika into your diet – it's a very good source of Thiamin and Magnesium'. How do you do that then? Make paprika pie? Sprinkle it on chips?

5. It's not just kelp that the eager disciple must learn how to swallow, it's self-help bullcrap as well. Gillian McKeith recommends inhaling and exhaling (which is, to be fair, sound advice). While repeatedly saying 'I love me' (which is more like tosspot advice). Plus, there's her 'little secret': five minutes jumping up and down on a trampette. While, presumably, screaming: 'I give myself the horn! I give myself the horn!'

6. All nutritionists try outdoing each other to be most foam-flecked fundamentalist of them all. Dr John Briffa (who, amazingly, is a real doctor) said: 'Breakfast cereals such as Weetabix, All-Bran and Alpen have had generally good publicity from the dietetic establishment, but I have my doubts . . .' Oh, so you have your doubts about bran-based cereals? And are these serious doubts? Public-health-warning-level doubts? Or the kind of doubts that nobody really needs to hear about? Silly twat.

7. All proper food advisers see dinnertime as a Manichean struggle between good and evil. Red meat? Hear the demons hissing. Alfalfa sprouts? All the birds have started singing. Lovely, isn't it? Except that, confusingly, the forces of 'good' are represented by Gillian McKeith cackling away on her trampette with bundles of wheatgrass stuffed into her ears.

8. Even the government's advice is fairly peculiar: eat five to nine pieces of fresh fruit or veg a day. What happens if you have 10? Do they all start jostling each other inside your system, the berries ganging up on the bananas and having drive-by shootings inside your stomach? Certain combinations of fruit were used in the war to produce bombs, and if eaten will cause instant immolation.

9. Where were we?

10. Oh yes, and they really are total freaks (let's be clear about this). Gillian McKeith's book *You Are What You Eat* has a whole chapter on the wrong kind of stools – some people, apparently, even suffer from 'FOUL-SMELLING STOOLS'. Imagine that! Every member of the public who appeared on her programme had to undergo an enema, the results of which would then be studied with interest by McKeith. Weirdly, at no point in the series did anyone say: 'Hang on, I'm on national telly letting a freak prod around in my poo. What has become . . . of *me*?'

Football buyouts

Here is a fun quiz.

1. Given that Malcolm Glazer's guzzling-up of Man Utd will see the club saddled with the sort of debt that would bankrupt the Bank of England, should we:
    a) Laugh. It's Man Utd.

b) Appreciate that it is sound market sense. Or as *The Economist* put it: 'As United tickets are now underpriced (rampant ticket-touting surely indicates unmet demand), [Glazer] can and arguably should raise prices. If some fans then boycott United games, as they say they will, there are lots more where they came from.'

c) Cry. Glazer's going to finish off English football as anything other than the plaything/cashcow of a load of billionaires, starting by ending collective bargaining over TV rights so big clubs get all the money and West Brom, say, never get on the telly. (Hmm . . . no, that is definitely bad. Moment of madness.)

d) Okay, it is a bit funny. Even though it is Really Bad.

2. In 2004, Libyan leader Colonel Gaddafi expressed a desire to buy Crystal Palace. Would that be:

a) A good thing. He seems like a nice guy. I like his hats and his zany sense of humour.

b) A bad thing. Fucking hell, why not flog Newcastle to Mugabe and Birmingham City to the Phoenix Four and let the whole league become a giant version of the popular world domination board game Risk. Bollocks to it, let's just give up on the whole fucking charade and get into the darts instead. Live from the Lakeside? I'll say.

c) It's a trick question and Crystal Palace doesn't exist, not even as an area of south London or as a big greenhouse full of steam engines during the Great Exhibition of 1851, which didn't happen either.

3. Where did Roman Abramovich get his money? Did he:

a) Find it on a bus. He handed it in but after an investigation no one claimed the money so the bus company said it was 'morally his'.

b) Marry John Kerry's wife, the one with all the Heinz beans money.

c) Pull off a 20p, 128-horse accumulator, including the famous Glorious Goodwood victory of 250-1 outsider Horsey.

d) Get it by 'talking gullible workers out of their share vouchers, making billions out of rigged privatisations, associating with share dilution coups and the like', and by 'slashed wages' for Siberian oil workers and 'shameless, albeit legal, tax avoid[ance]' (Dominic Midgley, and Chris Hutchins, *Abramovich: The Billionaire from Nowhere*). Thus Abramovich has accumulated oil-barrelsful of lolly as one of the most enduring Russian oligarchs – the breed of ruthless free-marketeers summed up generally to Midgley and Hutchins by a seasoned 'Moscow Watcher' thus: 'All these guys are kind of barracudas'.

Marshall I. Goldman says that of all the Russian oil companies' efforts to avoid being taxed, it was always Abramovich's Sibneft that 'paid the least' (Goldman, *The Piratization of Russia*). Sibneft controls the vast Siberian oilfield, which is the size of Wales; Yeltsin offloaded it to his mates Abramovich and former mentor Boris Berezovsky in an 'auction' where the only bidders were companies owned by Berezovsky and Abramovich 'for less than $200m [a fraction of its true value] . . . by the end of 2003 [it] was valued at $15 billion' (Midgley and Hutchins). The Siberians who might have thought they were going to benefit from that mineral wealth, what with having put up with Stalinism and all, may well wonder what it's doing running around a south-west London football stadium in a blue shirt. Tax avoidance ruses have included, once Abramovich became Governor of the oil-rich province of Chukotka, registering lots of his companies there and then using his new powers to 'grant large tax breaks' to them (Peter Truscott, *Putin's Progress*). 'Tax cut, Mr Abramovich?' 'I don't mind if I do, Mr Abramovich . . .'

However one evaluates the vagaries of the Russian tax system, it is undeniable that the money Abramovich throws about on yachts, jets, Kensington mansions and enough world-class players to, as Jose Mourinho commented at the start of the 2005/6 season, field two equally good whole teams who could defend the Premiership title, came from publicly owned resources bought for nix in a country of immense poverty. All in all, we might concur with Will Buckley in the *Observer*, précising a BBC documentary that attempted to unpack the Russian doll structure of Abramovich's empire (companies inside companies inside companies), that Abramovich's dealings at the very least 'lack . . . transparency'.

Personally, I find Chelsea fans being led by John Terry and Frank Lampard in chants of 'Roman Abramovich! Roman Abramovich!' to the tune of *'La donna e mobile'* when they won the title as depressing as them chanting their appreciation of privatisation. Or Putin. Or barracudas (not the fish).

e) It's a trick question and he hasn't got any money.

Now complete this tiebreaker: 'The Premiership is a load of stitched-up dogs' cock because . . .'

Football gofers

'Some people describe me as a Jim'll Fix It,' says Manchester United's player liaison officer Barry Moorhouse. 'I call myself a gofer. If [the players] want something done, I organise it.'

A more succinct definition would be 'servant'. Apart from ensuring players don't miss dentists' appointments and important promotional photo shoots, football gofers arrange houses for them, golf matches, flights, plumbers or – for foreign players moving to the UK – a National Insurance number, TV licence and bank account. They even go round and change lightbulbs. Also they iron players' newspapers (or copy of *Zoo*) and wipe their shitty arses with swan feathers. Probably.

When Fernando Hierro moved from Real Madrid to Bolton, gofers Matt Hockin and Sue Whittle not only put his kids into a local private school, they got adjoining flats for his family and his housekeeper (his personal bodyguard said he didn't need a flat, he'd sleep in the garden and eat moss (possibly)). They also had the premises furnished and sent a van to pick up a fridge-freezer from Comet. Plus they got Hierro an iPod and a laptop, and sorted him out with a bank account and council tax payment book.

The Spaniard still had one more request, says Hockin: 'He wanted to know where he could buy fresh fish and meat, so we took him to Bolton Market one day and said, "Here you go." He speaks English, so he's gone back since on his own and been absolutely fine.'

So, a grown adult 'managed to buy some fish'. He can buy fish *and* do a sliding tackle? Truly, he is a prince among men.

Except, even with the gofers, he is not treated as a prince. In fact, the whole gofer concept often falls woefully short. Do the gofers actually bow and scrape? (How does one actually scrape?) And do they refer to the player by their correct title – viz. 'my liege'? Are the players carried about in sedan chairs? And, if not, why not? These are busy people – busy, busy, busy. They have to run around for almost two entire hours of a morning. And they have to work on Saturdays.

Premiership footballers are also, objectively, better than the rest of us – like a 4-4-2 formation of Platonic philosopher kings. Are their shorts of purest silk and their boots of finest gold? Have they each an army of mighty and ruthless vassals sent into the local community to beat the locals and extract due tribute in the form of coin? Why fucking not?

And what of the constitutional issues? At the moment, the constitution places the Queen as ultimate arbiter of power. In theory, as head of the government and the judiciary and commander-in-chief of the armed forces, this feudal relic can dissolve Parliament and impose her will on her subjects. But has the Queen ever curled a free kick in from 30 yards? I've never seen her do it. I think it would be more satisfactory all round if Frank Lampard had the job.

For Lampard and St George! Or that goalie everyone called Safe Hands.

Foot spas

According to a recent survey, by October 2004 Britons had spent £450 million on foot spas. One in five adults owned one – but not a single one had ever been used (probably). Don't ask me who the fuck works this out or why – maybe it's what the people who set pub quizzes do in the daytime? – but it was in a newspaper so possibly a fact.

But at what point did these people feel they might need something full of hot water to put their feet in that wasn't the bath? Or, if you must, a bowl? It's like using the normal sink to wash your hands but having another, special basin just in case you fancy giving your pits a bit of a rinse.

Other useless items filling up people's cupboards include sandwich toasters and breadmakers. We've got £3.1 billion in useless goods under our collective stairs. What amazing fucking idiots we are. Stick that lot on eBay all in one go and we could probably bring down the economy.

Three-quarters of adults admitted having spent an average of £73 on such items. Presumably the other quarter are the ones who sold it to them and are sitting on a beach in the Maldives laughing like drains. Also, that's the average: so, if, say, 40 people only wasted a fiver, some poor bastard's got £2720 of shitty, useless tat to deal with. That's a lot of trouser presses.

Sandwich toasters are foul, Satanic tempters. They seem like a great idea right up to the point you produce your first cheese toastie and the cheese is hot enough to kill you and melts a hole in your hand.

Breadmakers are just complete and utter bastards. You assemble the eight trillion ingredients and leave it overnight as instructed – to be lulled to sleep by what sounds like someone being beaten senseless by a marine all night long. Look, it was a fucking present, all right, and we smashed it with a hammer and threw it out of an upstairs window. I'd advise you to do the same.

Forewords by Michael Palin

Everyone likes Palin. Michael Palin is a nice man. He's Vic and Bob's favourite Python, but equally he's probably also John Major's favourite Python. It is an iron law of history, and an actual law, passed by Parliament, that *everyone* likes Palin.

You've only got to put the word 'Palin' on a book and it'll fly out of the shops. This is why Michael Palin is asked to write forewords for more than 70% of all books published. He accepts approximately 97% of these solicitations, finding himself unable to say 'no' to all but the authors of books that slag off trains, mountains, great train journeys or travelling in general.

He's done forewords for things you might expect, like *The Traveller's Internet Guide* by Jonathan Lorie and Amy Sohanpaul, but he's also done forewords for books about *Viz* and *Dad's Army*. Plus he's done *Rail for the Future: An RDS Development Strategy*; *Football Days*, a handsome collection of Peter Robinson footie photies; *The Best of Southwold*, a collection of writings and photographs relating to the small Suffolk town of Southwold; *The Line That Refused to Die* by Stan Abbott and Alan Whitehouse, which is presumably about a particularly resilient line; and *Stammering: A Practical Guide for Teachers and Other Professionals*.

Palin even did a foreword for a book of his own limericks, under the pseudonym A. J. Gumby. Michael Palin is such a nice man he can't even say 'no' to himself. How nice is that? That's *very* nice.

Then there's: *S&M for Dummies*; Haynes' manual for the 1994 Nissan Micra; *Better Graph Design* by Professor Erno Erno Erno Erno Erno; and *Why Does No One Eat Turnips Any More? They Should, Because They're Nice* by Dave 'The Turnip' Turnip.

Former Presidents of the NUS

What have Jack Straw, Charles Clarke, David Aaronovitch, Trevor Phillips and Stephen Twigg got in common?

Yes, that's right, they are. But they are also all former Presidents of the National Union of Students.

As a student, Aaronovitch was a member of the Communist Party – the proper Soviet-sponsored one that thought Stalin was a sensible man and that the Russian invasion of Czechoslovakia was 'really good'. Now Aaronovitch goes round saying Blair is a sensible man and that the Iraq War is 'really good'. So, that's progress.

In latter years, NUS Presidents have not even waited until leaving office to embrace Blairism. So when former President Lorna Fitzsimons – who was a New Labour loyalist MP before being turfed out in 2005 – told the *Guardian* that 'all six ex-NUS presidents in Parliament are in favour [of top-up fees]', this should not have come as a shock. Was it a measure of the rightness of the government? A coincidence? Or possibly the reason they became MPs?

The late-90s, when Labour were flushing free education down the toilet like something dirty they never wanted to see again, saw the amazing spectacle of the Labour-led NUS refusing to organise national demonstrations against tuition fees. More strictly, of course, it was a non-spectacle – but none the less spectacular for that. Now these people are in Parliament or in extremely well paid jobs with New Labour's favourite companies. Yes, it probably is a coincidence.

Still, the Labour careerists are slightly better than certain elements in student politics, like the young man who calls himself Beany-Man and gets himself pictured in a bath of beans. Or the rugby-loving girl who has the vaguely titillating slogan 'Giving you what you want' and gets huge prop forwards to hand out leaflets like they might break your legs. Or the slightly touched and spooky mature student with one, very specific manifesto commitment relating to on-campus parking. Or the bloke who thinks 'if there's a Women's Officer there should be a Men's Officer – or, it's just, like, sexist'.

By the way, were you still up for Twigg? I wasn't.

Fraudulent race-against-time deadlines on TV shows

'Hang on, what's the flaming hurry?'

'Erm . . . well. Nothing, really. Just, you know . . . it makes things more tense. And we won't be able to shout things like Wow, I can't believe you painted those seven walls and converted that canal into a home for the blind, all in seven minutes – the drinks are on me!"

'Oh.'

'Funky', the word, as applied to anything except a musical genre

A Cityboy being shown around a sleek urban bachelor pad, on spying a particular 'feature', will say: 'Yah, funky. Okay.' Stripped pine bar-clubs filled to bursting with vacuous ball-aches will call itself The Funky Monkey. A new handbag with a slightly unusual buckle? That's funky. So too is a reasonably colourful mug.

So forget any earlier associations (adj. from the French *'funquer'* meaning 'to give off smoke' through to 'being enticingly odorous' and on to 'being rhythmically badass'). Now we must presumably imagine James Brown backsliding across some varnished floorboards holding a chrome cafetière and going: 'Urrgh!' With Funkadelic all sitting on little stools behind the breakfast bar.

And how 'funky' is that?

G

Gadget bores

William Morris said you should have nothing in your home that is not either beautiful or useful. So I wonder what he would make of boring bastards crapping on about their new sat-nav handheld spazz-top.

GADGET BORE: Look, it shows you all the streets and tells you where to turn.

WILLIAM MORRIS: But you've been doing that journey every weekday for four years. You already know the way. Also, this wallpaper's a bit shit.

GADGET BORE: Shows you where the nearest shoe shops are. You know, for if you need, erm, laces. Do you want to see my iPod playlist?

WILLIAM MORRIS: Cobblers to your iPod playlist. That IKEA table? It's bollocks.

If further proof were needed that electronic gizmos are just a way of filling the void, it is that the magazine for gadget bores is called *Stuff*. That's not even a proper name. What are you interested in? Stuff. That's just stupid.

Mecca for gadget bores is Akihabara in Tokyo – or 'Electric Town' – which the guidebooks describe as a dense maze of neon straight out of *Blade Runner* with electronic widgets so amazing you will probably want to sign up to be turned into an android.

However, if you go to Akihabara, you will find it's more like a really, really big branch of Dixon's where everything is in Japanese. The mutating neon could usefully all carry the slogan NOTHING TO SEE HERE. New mobile phones that aren't out here yet? Guess what: they look just like mobile phones that are out here yet. That is, not, at the end of the day, when it comes down to it, very interesting at all.

Later, emerging into a dimly lit sidestreet, you will almost be run over by what looks like a Japanese Nick Cave driving the smallest car you have ever seen.

Geographically inaccurate racism

At school, pop sensation Darius would get called 'Saddam'. In fact, his father is Iranian – only one letter and one very long war away from accuracy.

Radio One Asian DJ Nihal once got sent a charming picture with words 'Go back to India' written on with an arrow pointing to the Indian in the picture. The picture, carefully snipped from a magazine, portrayed a Peruvian Indian.

If people do have to be racist, do they also need to be so droolingly braindead that they can't tell which ethnic group they are rabidly insulting? Maybe they should make special racist maps.

Glastonbury toffs

You've just queued for three and a half hours to shit out your £8 botulism burger plus most of your innards, having navigated your way through a herd of tripping hippies, and now you are standing, at great personal financial expense, in the pissing rain, approximately four miles from a stage on which there is Rod fucking Stewart. You're living the fucking dream all right, but at least it can't get any worse. But then, here it comes, carried by the chilly breeze, *precisely* the sort of fucking cunt you came here to get away from, the braying cry of the acid toff: 'Tim! Tim!'

These are well-brought-up young men and women from the Home Counties who like to consider themselves part of dance music's one love family despite having a trust fund and a father with an entry in *Debrett's*.

They like dance acts with a woolly, *Lonely Planet*-guide message of spiritual uplift, especially if they boast a) a bongo solo, b) multiple vocalists who spend a lot of time grinning at each other, or c) an opportunity for the crowd to throw up their hands and shout 'peace'. A bit of hip-hop too, but only if it has a 'positive' attitude, i.e., it sounds a bit like De La Soul. And Groove Armada. Obviously.

They use 'funky' as a blanket term of approbation. (See **Funky, the word**.) They have annoying euphemisms for drugs, like 'ganj'. They return from far-flung places with starry-eyed tales of super-strength marijuana gifted them by a kindly old Tibetan, before taking up jobs in advertising and management consultancy, where, newly shorn of all that fucking hair, they vacuum up lines of cocaine as thick as railway tracks. They don't like talking about politics or anything else which might imperil their 'vibe', especially because they grew up in one of the safest Tory seats in England. They know what it's like to endure a comedown while on a Countryside Alliance march. They are in fact one of the few arguments in favour of hunting with dogs, but not in the way they intended.

Global warming sceptics

If you're worried about global warming, you must be some kind of pussy. The ice caps aren't melting. There aren't more forest fires or old people dying in heatwaves. The seas aren't getting substantially warmer – and even if they are, which they aren't, the fish are absolutely loving it!

We know this because of a small cabal of scientists who believe in big business more than life itself and who, funnily enough, often receive funding from ExxonMobil. These 'sceptics' get everywhere: by the President's ear; near to big business; on news programmes keen to stir up 'debate' and show they're not biased against frothing nutjobs.

In 2004, Myron Ebell, a director at the Competitive Enterprise Institute, told Radio 4's *Today* programme that global warming fears were 'ridiculous, unrealistic and alarmist' and that European countries were 'not out to save the world, but out to get America'.

In 2005, White House official – and former oil industry lobbyist – Philip Cooney was found to have filed reports on the link between greenhouse gases and climate change with dozens of amendments that all exaggerated scientific doubts. That was before he left the White House for a job with . . . ExxonMobil! Could you make it up? Probably, but there's no need.

All this despite the fact that virtually all other climatologists – the ones without links to the fossil fuels industry – now predict that even a conservative rise of 2.1 degrees will probably result in tens of millions of people losing their lives. Even a suppressed Pentagon report warned of a danger that far outstripped terrorism, mega-droughts, famine. Thanks to a newly submerged Gulf Stream, by 2020 the British climate could rival Siberia's. Thankfully, President Bush responded immediately. By standing proud alongside the British PM and declaring: 'We need to know more about it.'

More about what? You can see how this thing will develop in years to come . . . But Myron, I've just put a page of A4 paper in sunlight and watched it spontaneously combust. 'Sheer alarmism – we've always had hot days!' But Myron, a herd of gazelles has just elegantly pranced past the window of our London studio. 'Er, yes, they're mine. I brought them along with me especially. That big one – he's called Dave and he likes crisps.'

And Myron, now you're being swept into the skies by a freak tornado. 'What a funny thing you are! I see nothing extraordinary in this turn of events . . . It's great up here! Hi George, good to see you! Pretty breezy, I know! You what? You want to know more about it? It's okay, I'm on it!!'

Golden Age of Policing, the

Dixon of Dock Green (and I really can't stress this highly enough) was – not – real. He – was – made – up – by – the – telly.

So, if you are working on a news programme and want to put some historical perspective on anything to do with the police, it really is not acceptable to refer to or show a clip of this made-up bobby – even if he is whistling 'Maybe It's Because I'm A Londoner'.

See also Santa Claus, the Tooth Fairy, the Tweenies.

Gravity-defying cream

Clinique's Anti-Gravity Firming Lift Cream is marketed to women as preventing the inevitable downward effects of the ageing process: 'A lightweight oil-free formula [it] helps firm up skin instantly and over time [helping] to erase the look of lines as it tightens. Anti-Gravity Firming Lift Lotion by Clinique restores supple cushion to time-thinned skin.'

Of course it does.

Things known to science to defy gravity: aeroplanes, missiles, space rockets. Things known to science to not, generally speaking, defy gravity: magazines, biscuits (not even very light wafers), trousers, cream.

Gravy train, the

Transport laid on for bastards by The Man.

Not to be confused with: the gravy boat, which is laid on by Your Mam; 'Love Train', which was laid down by the O'Jays.

To be confused with: Virgin Trains.

Philip Green

All business reports concerning 'the high street' have to mention Philip Green at least twice. Why do I know who Philip Green is? He owns BHS. So what? He may buy M&S. Or he may not. So what?

At the end of the day, he's just some rich bloke who owns a lot of shops: but this is not interesting. Neither is it news: 'BONG! Rich bloke owns shops.' See? Rubbish.

For some reason, though, the media is obsessed with telling us the behind-the-scenes action on the high street, as if it were a soap opera or remotely interesting in some way. Christmas 2004 saw us constantly updated on whether today was a 'good' or 'bad' day on the high street – as if Christmas would be utterly ruined for us all if Debenhams' profits were slightly lower than expected.

Sainsbury's dip in the share of the groceries market also provided endless fascination, with company spokespeople obliging media efforts to make the dull interesting by referring to their efforts to sell some more stuff as a 'dogfight', as if they were just a hair's breadth away from launching a squadron of Lancasters to fire-bomb Morrison's.

The thing is, who fucking cares? Even if one high-street chain does close, so what? Another will open in its place. There is not going to be any shortage on the high street of bastards hawking tat – of that we can be fairly sure.

If you are interested, there is a readily available source: the *Financial Times*. But really, don't bother, it's incredibly tedious. Quite considerably, they even print it on different coloured paper so you don't wander into a newsagent's and mistake it for something interesting.

Guinness Book of World Records, the

Genuine Guinness world records include making the World's Largest Dog Biscuit or constructing the Fastest Thirty-Level Jenga Tower. Why not just go for the World's Single Most Pointless Individual Obsessively Engaged in a Heart-Sinkingly Futile Act?

The Guinness world record for holding the most Guinness world records is held by Ashrita Furman of New York – including Longest Milk Bottle Head Balancing Walk. This fucking freak walked 130.3 kilometres with a fucking milk bottle on his empty fucking head.

Furman also holds the Milk Crate Balancing On Chin record, the Fastest Pogo Stick Jumping Up The CN Tower record, and the Orange Nose Push – Fastest Mile record (24 min 36 sec. Woo! Woo!). Since the 1970s, he has set more than 80 Guinness world records. As of November 2004, he held 20: this means that people see these pointless records and then aspire to break them; presumably saying things like '434 games of hopscotch in a 24-hour period? Ea-sy!'

Ashrita puts his amazing success down to his daily meditation regime. After discovering the spiritual teachings of Sri Chinmoy, he renamed himself Ashrita in 1974. His real name is Keith (you couldn't actually make this up). guinnessworldrecords.com explains: 'Ashrita is on a spiritual mission and uses his inner spirit to perform the record-breaking feats. Under the instruction of his guru he says he's been able to attain a new level of self-transcendence – meaning he can overcome the physical pain and mental anguish of his testing record attempts.'

Didn't fancy using your 'inner spirit' and 'self-transcendence' for, say, the attainment of world peace then, Keith? At least Furman merits inclusion in the book. So many people are setting world records that many don't even get a mention. Imagine that: you've just set the record for the Longest Wank In A Bath Of Beans, and it's not even in the book. How are you going to feel then?

The book – the highest-selling copyright title of all time, at more than one hundred million copies (haven't all these people considered going for a walk or something?) – was set up (in the 1950s) and edited by Norris McWhirter (with his brother Ross), who was not far off being a fascist. He was forever attacking CND, funding strike-breakers and defending sportspeople who went to South Africa during apartheid.

A rabid anti-European, McWhirter was caught altering the 1975 edition book proofs just before they were sent to the printers, adding: 'World's Best Country: England' and 'World's Worst Country: the Boche'.

Also, more seriously, he was responsible for long-running children's programme *Record Breakers*. Which featured far, far too much tap-dancing.

H

Handball

People would take the Olympics a lot more seriously if they didn't include handball. They're just throwing a ball to each other like a bunch of kids. It's just stupid.

And if you win, how do you look, say, the marathon gold medallist in the eye? . . .

HANDBALL GOLD MEDALLIST: What did you get your gold for?

MARATHON GOLD MEDALLIST: I ran 26 miles in extreme heat.

HANDBALL GOLD MEDALLIST: Great. I threw a ball back and forth for a bit with someone about two feet away from me. Then I had a bath.

MARATHON GOLD MEDALLIST: Big twat.

'Hard-working families'

All through the 2005 election campaign, there was only one kind of family that mattered: one with its nose constantly rubbing against the grindstone.

At the 2004 Labour conference, Tony Blair set out his stall, envisaging 'a 21st century Britain . . . where hard-working families who play by the rules are not going to see their opportunities blighted by those that don't'.

But, but . . . I didn't know there were rules about working hard. Why didn't you tell me earlier?

A better life awaits if you continue jumping through the hoops, ideally only popping home after work for 15 minutes before taking out your minicab all night. After that, feel the satisfaction of helping provide – to quote the other main conference slogan – 'A Better Future For All'. It's a poignant, beautiful idea.

No it's not! This never happens! Not ever! Not even one time! In reality, families who work so hard they barely see each other mainly provide better futures for divorce lawyers, builders of one-bed accommodation and breweries who do tinnies. Considering Blair's ideas about pushing the working age up to 70, it unfortunately looks like there's gold at the end of the rainbow like there's gold at the end of your arse.

Work your little mittens off and not only will you on average earn about a fifth of what Blair earns (never mind Cherie), you won't get a free holiday courtesy of Cliff Richard or Silvio fucking Berlus-fucking-sconi. You'll also find that if you work really, really hard it often only leads to a future of working even harder than that, because employers tend to be greedy bastards who see a soft touch coming a fucking mile off.

I'm sure I read somewhere once that the job of the government was to look after the interests of the general populace – which would presumably include such things as making sure they didn't have to work too hard at the behest of some unscrupulous bastard. Apparently not: it's the job of government to make the general populace help big business and the very rich. It's only fair.

With this is mind, we have produced a pledge card for

hard-working families. It's like the ones New Labour knock out at election time except it's in English and, unlike theirs, if you don't keep the promises, you go to prison. It includes things like having the decency to die before drawing a pension and leaving your wordly goods to SmithKline Beecham.

Hare Krishnas
Hare, hare krishna
Hare hare
Hare bollocks
Bollocks
Bollocks krishna
Hare bollocks
Bollocks hare
(REPEAT)

'Having one of those days?' advertising
Having one of those days? Someone at the office giving you the hump? Got rained on at lunch? Hair? Him? And that?

Don't worry, girls. Just relax on a big, snuggly sofa with a steaming mug of hot chocolate (lo-cal, natch!) and think about scrummy guys, etc., etc. With adverts for products aimed primarily at females aged 20–35, you can virtually hear the brains of lumpen creatives filling in the cliché boxes with a big lazy tick: okay . . . vulnerable, likes snuggling up, 'having one of those days?', shake it all off with . . . bubbles, thinking about scrummy guys, lo-cal hot chocolate . . . pamper pamper, more hot chocolate, mmmm, steamy and warm, mmmm, bubbles, luxuriant bubble bath absolutely everywhere . . . 'having one of those days?' . . . more bubbles. Candles!

Bish bash bosh. Right! Lunchy?

Health-food entrepreneurs

Wholemeal breadheads.

Henmania

In June 2004, Tim Henman proudly ran through the grounds at Wimbledon with the Olympic torch, which was being carried through London en route to Athens.

Henman took the flame from Sir Roger Bannister, whose last words to the British number one were: 'Make sure you don't drop it.' Even septuagenarian sporting legends, on seeing Henman, think: twat.

Every year we have to go through the same bastard charade. Shitloads of hoorays camp out at Wimbledon going 'Wah!', painting their faces with the St George's Cross and exhorting Timmy to 'do it for England' – then, very shortly after, in fact it feels like it might only be hours later, he crashes out of the tournament – possibly to the 152nd best player in the world.

Any rational observer would say that Henman's failure to win Wimbledon is perfectly understandable considering that he is 'quite good' at tennis as opposed to 'really, really good' at tennis. But to the Henmaniacs, that strange tribe of posh freaks who make the Last Night of the Proms look like 'a laugh', Henman's annual Wimbledon appearance seems to constitute the sun going back up on the Empire.

Revealing their surplus stupidity, during a match at the 2005 Australian Open, a large group of Henmaniacs were shouting 'Do it for Chiswick!' As Tim himself pointed out: 'I don't live in Chiswick.'

But what will become of Tim? The Henmaniacs can wash the face paint off and drown their sorrows in the nearest All Bar One. They'll have forgotten about it by tomorrow. They'll have forgotten most things by tomorrow. But what of their hero? Will Timmy be up all night, mulling over what might have been, drowning his pain in tumbler after tumbler of Robinson's Barley Water?

Never mind, with all that charisma he's a shoo-in for a commentating job on the Beeb.

Lady Isabella Hervey

Being famous for being Lady Victoria Hervey's sister? Are there scales for this sort of thing? Truly, I hope not.

High-profile local businessmen

Every town has one: the local boy made good who always has his face in the local papers and plastered over buses. And it's always carpets, for some reason. He drives around like the king of the world, when he is in actuality the king of low-cost carpet retail in south Leeds, which isn't the same thing.

The nation's foremost high-profile local businessman is possibly Bruce Robertson of Trago Mills, the chain across Devon and Cornwall that resembles pound shops taking over an aircraft hangar. Bruce's father, Mike, who founded the

Trago empire, had gargoyles made of local and national politicians he didn't like. Upholding this proud family tradition, Bruce supports imperial weights and measures by putting big boards up outside Trago stores saying 'Brussels be damned, We sell sprouts by the lb'. He has been, perhaps unsurprisingly, a major funder of UKIP.

Bruce has even paid for advertorials in the local paper putting forward his singular points of view. In 1988, one screed was censured by the Advertising Standards Authority for inciting homophobic violence: he advocated 'the castration of all homosexual perverts' – presumably with a pair of Trago-purchased shears. So, Trago is unlikely to be selling discount buttplugs anytime soon.

Reflecting the Robertsons' popularity among local people, when the Newton Abbot Trago Mills store went up in smoke in October 2004, e-mails flooded into the BBC Radio Devon website.

Nick from Brixham said: 'I'd heard the fire has caused £5 million of improvements. I suppose the charcoal barbecue bricks section will do a roaring trade in the next few weeks.'

Peter from Exeter added: 'Poor old Trago. I was very familiar with the store. Shame it happened. On another note, if anyone has any interest in buying 500 fake Xmas trees – slightly blackened – then I'll be at Marsh Barton carboot this Sunday.'

James from Newton Abbot reckoned: 'I used to work there and it was rubbish.'

Ames, meanwhile, had clearly conducted some sort of survey: 'Everyone I have spoken to is really pleased the place has burnt down.'

And after everything Brucie had done for the local community, too. Presumably it's all a conspiracy by uncastrated gay Boche?

Hip hotels

Hip hotels might have boxy rooms, bad beds and shrill staff seemingly beamed in from another planet. But there's a great selection of Latin chill CDs.

- At Milan's über-trendy Hive Hotel, beekeeping is the theme. Visitors can join in the beekeeping themselves or just relax, put their feet up and let the staff take care of the bees.
- At Notting Hill's boutique hotel BŒulk, they've got an eight-year-old girl on a swing. Sometimes she sings 'Son Of A Preacherman'. Sometimes not.
- Every room in West Hollywood's Barker Ranch features a mural of a different member of the Manson family rendered in the blown-up-cartoon style of Roy Lichtenstein. Sheets are flecked with fake blood. To further resemble a cult of homicidal White Power hippies, all staff have tiny swastikas tattooed on to their foreheads (guests can get their own done too).
- Berlin's superb Hotel Hostel has knocked away the interior walls so guests effectively sleep in unisex dorms. Around the clock, the kitchen staff offer classic hostel fare like sausage 'n' beans and macaroni cheese.

The word 'hip' is actually believed to derive from the Wolof (the dominant language in Senegal) word 'hipi' meaning 'to open one's eyes' or 'to be aware'.

Of course, anyone who truly opens their eyes and becomes aware while staying at a hip hotel might well be moved to declare: 'I have just become completely aware that I am being totally fleeced for a poky room, crap service and decor that's like the imaginings of a pretentious mental case.'

Homophobic Christians

Casting around for the one true path in life, Christians often ask themselves: 'WWJD?' – 'What would Jesus do?' Apparently, he wouldn't 'make some stuff out of wood' or 'cure the sick', but would walk up and down the high street with a big placard reading 'GOD HATES FAGS'.

The 'Jesus as uptight, bigoted sociopath' reading of the Bible is proving incredibly popular with the world's rising band of evangelicals. Even the born-again movement's pre-eminent marketing arm The Alpha Course (which has seen over 1.5 million Brits pass through its doors) has raised heckles after Blairish founder Nicky Gumbel claimed the Bible 'makes it clear' that gays and lesbians need to be 'healed'. 'Although I strongly advise you not to say the word "healed" to them,' he once warned. 'They hate that word!' Sound advice.

Normal people flicking through The Good Book will find anti-gay sentiments quite tricky to unearth. The New Testament's supposed 'No To Homos' message basically boils down to Paul the Apostle's comments in Romans 1: 26–27 on the sins of the Gentiles – 'God gave them up unto shameful affections' – and depends on the translation of the mysterious Ancient Greek word *'arsenokoites'* (and I promise that's actually true) which might mean 'special gay friend' or possibly 'male temple prostitute' or even 'gigolo for rich women'. Now there's a solid bedrock for bigotry if ever we saw one.

For others, though, the Bible is just one big old book about hating queers; they're constantly finding startling new chapters like when Jesus, after healing the sick and helping the poor, draws together his disciples and tells them how God's vision embraces everyone – prostitutes, paupers, lepers, even tree-climbing tax inspectors . . . 'On hearing this, his disciples pauseth for a moment and said unto him, What about the gays, Lord? Jesus flincheth and spat, Oh no, not the gays. I don't like them, he ranteth. I don't like their white vests or their love of gaudy music. And I have it on the highest authority of a man down the tavern that there's a gay mafia running the Roman Empire. A man with another man? No way! Anyway, the lepers . . .'

In fact, the Big Bad Son Of God never mentions bum sex or any other gay-related issue even once, not even mutual masturbation. It's possible he planned on making his Big Speech Against The Gays right after Easter. We'll never know.

'Hot' collective cover shoots

Whenever magazines or colour supplements suffer crises of faith over whether they are still 'hot' or, in fact, 'not', they usually gather together a stellar array of undeniably hot, sometimes even hotter-than-hot, really actually quite burny-hot young things for a big old cover shoot that will jump off news-stands with an eye-grabbing headline like 'UK's Hippest Designers of Hip Stuff', '40 Hottest Writers Of Hot Books Under 40', 'The Hottest Human Rights Lawyers in Hotsville', 'The Britpack Take Off! Honestly! This Time It's True!',* or 'This Week's Hot Hollywood Hotties – In Their Hotpants!'

Inside, the editor's letter will say: 'Can you feel the heat? Hot off the presses, here's the latest hot young things – they're hot like hot cats on a hot tin roof, like inappropriately hot soup on a hot summer's day, like hot cakes, hot tubs, hot potatoes and those hot flannels you get in Chinese restaurants. Hot! If things were any hotter around here . . . oh, hang on . . . I appear to be melting . . . look at that, I'm actually melting! Aaaaargh!!!'

What everyone in these pictures should realise is that, as soon as the shutter clicks, they will start to cool. By the time they leave the studio, they will already only be 'warm'. In a year's time, nobody will remember even the slightest thing about them.

* Anyone partaking in a gathering referred to as a 'Britpack' might as well book an appointment with the DSS right away. Message to the world: the British aren't coming. Not now. Not ever.

Hotdesks

I can understand why you might want fewer desks than employees – to keep them 'motivated', that is, to create some kind of Hobbesian war of all against all, everyone doomed to insecurity and battling for scarce resources, never allowed to settle in one place and get the idea that they may have a job to come to tomorrow rather than being expelled at speed down a waste chute into a vacuum.

But do you have to make them hot as well? Is insecurity not enough that you have to fucking scald people? Jesus – actually burning your workers; it's positively barbaric.

I

IKEA

When IKEA opened its new store in Edmonton, security guards were soon swamped by 6,000 shoppers grabbing at sofas and shouting 'Mine! Mine!' Many collapsed with heat exhaustion and 20 needed hospital treatment.

Of course, we're not suggesting the company was in any way responsible for the carnage. After all, a visit to IKEA is usually connected in my mind with inner calm, low blood pressure and a total absence of any thoughts of violence. No, hang on – I was thinking of the park.*

IKEA fucks with your head. All you want is some furniture: why do they want your sanity in return? The layout alone makes you feel like a lab rat. The stores are like psychoactive jigsaw puzzles with moving pieces, designed by a sick Swedish physicist with access to extra dimensions.

They have what look like short cuts between adjoining sections, allowing you to pop through a little walkway from one part of the store to another. But where you end up won't be where you were trying to get to, even if the store map said it would be. Worse, if you decide you were better off where you were, and pop back through the hole, you won't end up where you started, but in a different section again. Sometimes on a different floor altogether. In a different branch of IKEA.

There are some amazing statistics concerning IKEA.

Apparently, 95% of all couples who move in together visit an IKEA within one month of moving in together. Of these, only 3% manage to buy the things they went there for, and 100% of them are related to the staff.

Young couples troop into IKEA with high hopes. They emerge as husks. And without having bought any furniture. IKEA still makes huge profits, however – all of which come from those funny Scandinavian hot dogs, meatballs and cakes they sell at the exit. And from light bulbs.

100% of people who visit IKEA buy light bulbs. IKEA do sell very cheap light bulbs. Everyone buys the light bulbs because a) they are so cheap, and b) they can't come away empty-handed having spent three hours of pain and panic in IKEA.

Everything in IKEA has funny names: you will find cupboards and beds called things like Dave and Philip, or Clare. Or Jurgen-Bergen-Heldenveldenstetser. If you try to buy any of them, you will be directed to a warehouse section where your item – a chair, say – is placed carefully on top of some 80-feet-high shelves. They will tell you that a man will come and get it down for you. The man will never come.

* Incidentally, news reports on the Edmonton madness invariably noted a stabbing incident nearby – which was actually just a stabbing incident nearby. But for some it brought home the reality of what had just happened. One customer was quoted as saying: 'I turned around for one moment and someone stole my sofa. But at least I'm alive.' That's true, but what about the cheap sofa?

Improving the value of your property

Houses aren't for living in, they're for making cash out of. A good kitchen in a £100,000 property can add 10%. The introduction of a classic bathroom, that might cost just £4,000, can instantly add £1 million to the asking price.

But it's easy for beginners to make mistakes, so here we recommend our Twenty Quick Ways Not To Improve The Value Of Your Home – which is possibly going to be shown on the telly in the new year:

1. Ruthlessly cut out all natural light with ripped up rubbish sacks over the windows.
2. Scatter pigs' entrails around the landing.
3. Put a big sign on the door saying: 'Jesus loves this house.'
4. Shit on the floor.
5. Open up the hallway as a public bridleway.
6. Pretend it's built upon an ancient American Indian burial ground.
7. Disappear into the loft. And never come down.
8. In the middle of the living room, build a little wooden town for a 15-strong mouse troupe to scurry about in. Call this Mouse Town.
9. Redirect the sewers in any way whatsoever – they're probably connected in the right way anyway.
10. Take in waifs and strays.
11. Replace your cooker with a tiny plastic one made for children that doesn't even have any connections for the gas/electrics.
12. Burn the fucker to the ground.

'Inner', the word

There was once presumably a time when the word 'inner' just referred to things that were not 'outer'. A bicycle's 'inner tube' was the ring of rubber that nestled snugly inside the outer rubber tyre. The bicycle never had to discover its inner tube, or nurture its inner tube, or even explore the cosmic dimensions of its inner tube. It was just an inner tube.

But something happened and the word 'inner' started implying a righteous quest towards the glowing centre of one's own glorious self. So now leaflets offer 'Creating Inner Freedom', local libraries offer titles like *The Inner Feng Shui: Using Ancient Chinese Art For Inner Development* and even *Mind of a Ninja: Exploring the Inner Power*. Companies like Inner Gifts offer inner knick-knacks to whack on your inner credit card including a skin-care range – using 'only the most potent, pure oils and organic or wild crafted botanicals in abundant concentrations for optimal results' – called, rather brilliantly, Kiss My Face.

A reiki retreat in Denver, Colorado – offering a Primordial Sound Meditation Class by a teacher 'certified by Deepak Chopra and Infinite Possibilities Knowledge' – calls itself The Inner Sanctum. Which does, at least, hint at the part of the human anatomy where such 'inner' beliefs originate.

The Intel Inside tune

The four Intel Inside chimes (da-da da-ding!) are played somewhere in the world on average every five minutes.

Intel (da-da da-ding!) commissioned Austrian musician Walter Werzowa (the evil genius behind 1988 yodel-house hit 'Edelwiss') in 1994 to compose a three-second jingle that 'evoked innovation, troubleshooting skills and the inside of a computer, while also sounding corporate and inviting'.

More than a jingle, this is a 'sonic logo' that coincides with every mention of 'Intel' (da-da da-ding!). Which leads to some terrifying sonic pile-ups like a recent PC World advert in which the initial glowsticks-aloft trance jolted into the Intel logo (da-da da-ding!) before cutting back to the trance and ending with the traditional: 'Where in the world? PC World!'

Wait till Intel gets outside. Then we'll be really fucked.

Interactive media

Seeing as the TV channels either get the licence fee or bombard us with a never-ending kaleidoscope of mind-numbing advertisements, and thus can by no means be considered skint, why aren't they paying professionals to make their programmes rather than asking me to fill in all the time? They are FOR-EVER canvassing my opinion on this, or getting me to speak out about that. E-mail us, they say, press the red button now, text, call in.

Why me? All I'm trying to do is watch the television, an activity I associate mostly with watching and listening and occasionally shouting and swearing and throwing crisps about, not sharing my opinions with an underwhelmed nation.

This is the very acme of modern democracy, though: don't bother going on a demonstration or writing to your MP, just text what's bothering you to *The Wright Stuff*. Same difference.

The programmes, by lazily reflecting back to us what we already know, can fill up time without having to go to the terrible trouble of getting people in who might, say, know what they're fucking talking about. Middle East road map irrevocably stalled? Just have a text poll; much easier than finding someone who could, say, identify Israel on a map. Don't worry about informing the viewers, they only want to see Z-list celebs wanking each other off anyway.

So, red buttons. Actually, no, while I think of it, 'shock-jock controversial radio phone-ins' – like John Gaunt on BBC London. That's public sector broadcasting, is it – an ill-informed fat bloke shouting at you?

And it doesn't matter how many times you and your mates press the red button during *Best Films Ever*, even if you run up a bill of £9,000: they will fiddle it and *Sex Lives of the Potato Men* will NEVER win.

Iraq War euphemisms

Having a great big war going on day after day requires a whole raft of new coinages to stop people from getting too hopelessly worked up about bodies falling apart and other things that really shouldn't concern them. The Iraq War has spawned a whole new range of such euphemisms to go alongside old favourites like 'friendly fire' and 'collateral damage'.

The whole affair was a 'preventive' or 'pre-emptive' war – a safety measure closer to fitting a smoke alarm to protect your home from the danger of fire – rather than, say, protecting your home from the danger of fire by launching missiles at it. It was also a 'war of choice' – as in 'car of choice' or 'cereal of choice' – which makes the coalition sound like a happy consumer rather than, say, the kind of consumer who bombs shops.

'Pacifying Fallujah' became an almost comfortably familiar

phrase (like 'Educating Rita' or 'Chasing Amy') – with its connotations of a dummy helping soothe a crying baby's distress. During the attack on Fallujah, the Foreign Office claimed displaced residents were 'visiting relatives' (presumably drinking too much tea with Derek Jacobs on in the background) and the Pentagon labelled the 10,000–15,000 universal soldiers helping interrogate/torture prisoners as 'private contractors'. Presumably, the word 'mercenary' sounded a bit, well, mercenary.

US news feeds would talk of another 'busy day in Baghdad' before going over to a correspondent who said, 'Yes, there's been some developments.' On one particular 'busy' day, 22 September 2004, the 'developments' included two US soldiers being accused of the cold-blooded murder of three Iraqi civilians, the discovery of the beheaded body of British hostage Jack Hensley, multiple car bombings causing 11 civilian deaths, plus a further 22 people killed in helicopter raids on Sadr City. So yes, definitely a 'busy' day. If you were living in Baghdad, you'd certainly come home saying: 'Busy out there today. Busy busy busy! There's what looks very much like a big fucking war going on.'

Perhaps next time we could do away with the word 'war' altogether and replace it with the words 'birthday party'. This will reinforce how coalition troops are calling in by invitation. On entering this 'party', we will start dropping 'cakes' on the hosts. Unfortunately, this might lead to some 'crumbs' falling on to the floor. But don't worry, because we'll wipe up any subsequent mess with 'tissues'. Lucrative oil and rebuilding contracts will be the 'sweets' we take home in our 'goody bag'.

Despite the invitations stating that the party ends at 4 p.m., we might stretch out the fun a little longer, possibly for some years.

ITV News Channel, the

What could be worse than ITV News? Twenty-four-hour, rolling ITV News, of course.

Amusingly, in January 2005 the BBC had a big panic when an internal survey found that ITV had more prime-time current affairs coverage than them. Then someone realised that they'd included *Tonight with Trevor McDonald* as current affairs and they all had a big laugh and a huge lunch on expenses.

J

Boris Johnson

Cheeky chappy Boris Johnson: is he quite amusing/a bit of a 'cove'/basically a 'good egg'? Or is he a Tory?

The case for Boris Johnson being a Tory:

- He's editor of the *Spectator*.
- He's a member of the Conservative Party.
- He's Conservative MP for Henley.

The case against Boris Johnson being a Tory:

- He's got floppy hair and he rides a bike.

Hmm. Tricky. But, oh, hang on: Tory MP – doesn't like asylum seekers – Brussels, blah blah – cut back welfare state and give money to the rich, blah blah . . .

Got it! He's a Tory! He's Nicholas Soames on a bike! Fooled us all! D'oh!

Dom Joly

Watch out, Britpop Beadle's about!

Juice drink

Juice: it is, almost by definition, a drink. Add the word 'drink' to the word 'juice' and you might imagine it becomes even more drinky, which is potentially delicious. But no.

If anything, it becomes less drinky. And it certainly becomes less juicy. In fact, your average 'juice drink' often contains a mere 10% juice; that's compared to the fulsome 100% juice that's always contained in 'juice'. Which should make people say things like: 'What happened there then? What did you do with all the juice?'

What if you needed to unwind after a hard day and fancied downing a bottle of tasty wine but the local off-licence only purveyed something called 'wine drink'; then, on returning home, you find the bottle contains just 10% of the wine of a normal bottle of wine (which is 100% wine) while the rest was just spit and rain?

You wouldn't be happy. You might not even get that pissed. And, when you start shouting about the whole matter outside your local off-licence, banging on the shuttered windows with your bloodied fists screaming 'Where is my fucking booze?', you'd definitely have justice on your side.

K

Kabbalah

Back when people imagined The Future on programmes like *Tomorrow's World*, the 21st century was full of jet-packs and robots doing your ironing. None of the so-called 'experts' predicted that everyone would be getting into a weird sect vaguely related to an ancient Jewish tradition that sells bits of red string to its followers at £18.50 a pop. Dr Heinz Wolff? You're a fucking charlatan.

Apparently, the reason that Madonna, Posh, Melinda Messenger et al. wear the red string is to protect them against 'the evil eye'. Seems a strange length to go to to stop people giving you dirty looks, but hey ho. Oh, and it gives you 'total fulfilment'.

Spreading 'total fulfilment' has been the aim of Philip Berg since he gave up his job as an insurance salesman in 1970 to become a bit of a seer. Called the Rav by followers, the American rabbi set up his first Kabbalah Centre in Israel in 1971. Clever marketing – and the 'donated' labour of followers – has seen that mushroom into 40 centres worldwide and a turnover of millions. By setting up both not-for-profit and private Kabbalah enterprises – plus wheezes like the Rav 'blessing' businesses in return for a cut of the profits – Berg and his wife Karen have managed to build up an enormous property portfolio and although they take no salaries have lavish no-expense-spared lifestyles for themselves and their two sons. The Rav sold a ten-year copyright to his books to the KC for over $2.5 million. That's a lot of red string.

The reason the string is so powerful, says the Rav, is that it has been wrapped seven times around Rachel's tomb on the West Bank. The people who run the tomb claim to have no knowledge of the Kabbalah Centre doing this, however, and the Israeli Ministry of Tourism and also for Religious Affairs have stated that no special permits have been given to the Kabbalah Centre to enter the heavily militarised area at Rachel's Tomb with large quantities of red string. In fact, the tomb dispenses its own type of red string; although presumably this contains much less enlightenment, what with it being completely free.

The Kabbalah Centre is even trying to get a patent on the red string. Presumably this will involve answering the question 'How long is a piece of string?' – so at least it'll finally clear up that old chestnut.

Other money-spinners include a set of the key Kabbalah texts, the Zohar, at £289. To achieve enlightenment, you don't even need to read the books – you can pick up their 'energy' by just tracing your finger over them. Ah, now I see why it's so attractive to pop stars.

A 1.5-litre bottle of Kabbalah water – which the Kabbalah Centre claims is 'purest Artesian' water which can cure cancer – will set you back £3.95. A case is £45. In fact, the water comes from a bottling plant in Canada.

Never mind all that, though; what about Madonna? According to a senior figure at the Kabbalah Centre in London quoted in the *Evening Standard*, Madonna joined to learn how to control her moods and 'how to be more tolerant with her husband'.

But I could have sorted that out for her, no $5 million dona-
tion required. He's an arsehole. It's not actually intolerant to
shout at him. I want to shout at him, and I've never met the
bloke: you fucking live with him, you freak.

Vernon Kay

Occasionally I have real fears about Vernon Kay taking over
the world. I find myself haunted by the thought of him pre-
senting all current-affairs television programmes, breaking off
from news stories to ask the viewers questions like: 'So, the
McCartney sisters: seriously, which one would you go for?
Sisters, eh? Eh? Wicked . . .'

I have visions of a future war with army-recruitment films
being shown constantly on giant screens in every home and
workplace and in public spaces across the town, featuring
Vernon Kay in a thumbs-up pose intoning: 'Right, guys! This
is serious, yeah?! Are you gonna do the right thing for your
country or WHAT?'

These fears might seem misplaced, even slightly mad. But
they are mine.

Keane

Keane need to be stopped, immediately, for these reasons:

- Singer Tom Chaplin's face has no edges, like runny
  cheese.
- The title of their debut album *Hopes And Fears* derives
  from the lyrics of 'O Little Town Of Bethlehem' which

is their favourite when they go carol-singing around their hometown of Battle. Their next album is called *Little Donkey (Carry Mary) ('Long the Dusty Road)*.

- Look at them! Just look at them!
- Speaking after the 2005 Brits, pianist Tim Rice-Oxley said: 'We went to an aftershow party given by our record company. I had a really good conservation with Jake from the Scissor Sisters, who I'd not met before. We did all get pretty pissed, I have to say.'
- Keane are not in any way related to Man Utd midfield hardman Roy Keane. Now that would be good: a piano-driven pop-rock outfit led by Roy Keane. Roy Keane repeatedly smashing his face against the piano keys and shouting: *that's* rock 'n' roll.
- Singer Tom Chaplin's face has no edges, like runny cheese.
- Understanding the importance of a 'consistent anchor', Keane got their own branding consultants – Moving Brands – before signing with their first label, together drawing up a list of buzz words including 'fascinating', 'innocent' and 'expansive'. When the band signed to Island, they absolutely insisted on retaining control over their branding. Forget about Roy Keane: *that's* rock n' roll.
- Singer Tom Chaplin's face has no edges, like runny cheese.
- Chaplin once claimed: 'There's always a strong, potent message to a Keane song. Whereas sometimes with Coldplay, you're not really sure what he's on about.' Which is only slightly less deluded than if he'd said: 'Hello, I'm Iggy Pop. Here's my big willy.'
- Just look at them! Again!

Ketamine

Having a bit of a dance? Don't trip over the a-hole in the k-hole.

Alicia Keys

Alicia Keys might well be the greatest soul singer of this or any other age. If the main premise of soul singing was to sound as conceited as possible.

Realising that what the world needed most was to share her innermost thoughts, this 'unbelievably talented' 'new Aretha' called her second album *The Diary Of Alicia Keys*. After that, she actually looked into publishing reworked versions of her teenage diaries from the age of nine onwards. At the time of writing, she was 'just formulating which style I want to write it in: straight based off my life or a little more journal-style in nature.'

In the meantime, she unleashed *Tears For Water: Songbook of Poems and Lyrics*, which featured reams of unused lyrics – because, according to her people, there are around a 'dozen unreleased [lyrical] gems for every song that makes it onto one of her albums'. Her introduction read: 'All my life, I've written these words with no thought or intention of sharing them . . .'

Even this was not enough to sate Keys' desire for Keys-related book product. Just try imagining the scene in the publisher's offices when she unleashed her finest idea: a young-adult detective series starring the 16-year-old Alicia as wannabe soul star who betrays a 'sometimes dangerous penchant for investigating – and solving – heart-pounding whodunits'. Bloody hell. What does she do? Go into bookshops and note down all the sections that don't have any books about Alicia Keys in?

Of course, it would be quite tragic if, at some point in the near future, the public unanimously decided that Miss Keys was not, after all, 'unbelievably talented' but really quite up herself and could, if she really wanted, go and spend the rest of her days in a cupboard. At that point, I would actually pay good money to read her innermost thoughts.

KFC

Why do you never see crusties and public schoolboys with scarves covering their mouths catapulting each other through the window of KFC? It's always McDonald's. But Colonel Sanders was a right bastard – just look at what he did to Elvis.

Robert Kilroy-Silk

Many people mock Robert Kilroy-Silk as a perma-tanned racist demagogue breathing molten horseshit, and laughed like drains when he was humiliated in the general election.

But, really, they could be a bit more compassionate. After all, Robert Kilroy-Silk is apparently being harassed, constantly, and in quite a serious way, by Muslims. And these are not peaceable Muslims, either. They are 'vicious Muslims'. Maybe they have knives? We just don't know.

Apparently, they are 'always' telling him what to do. They tell him what he can 'read, hear or say'. And that's a bit much. Maybe they ring him up? Or maybe they shout over the wall of his voluminous house at night? We just don't know.

They tell him what to read! But what? Judging by what comes out of his mouth, it's not an educative selection.

Now, Kilroy has made some stupid and offensive comments about the Middle East. But, come on – two wrongs don't make a right. Maybe if you left him alone to make up his own tiny mind – perhaps in a quiet shed – he would come up with something a bit less touched? We just don't know.

But shouting reading lists at him in the night is clearly not helping.

Kitsch tat shops

Called things like Missy Kitty Mau Mau or Puss Puss or Funky Monkey Pants. Sometimes the innocent shopper accidentally enters an emporium because they need to buy a present for someone and it claims to specialise in presents.

'Ooh,' they think. 'A present shop, maybe I can get a present in this shop for presents and thus satisfy my present-buying needs.' Then they go inside and remember that it's actually a festival of shit with price tags on. You can find:

- George Bush fridge magnets – you can dress him up as either Shirley Temple or Wonder Woman.
- A Monkey tape measure.
- Numerous cards featuring the picture of a 50s housewife and a rude slogan – something like, 'On Sundays, Doreen enjoyed nothing more than a good spit-roast'.
- A Wonder Woman cocktail shaker.
- A tiny little book about eating chocolate.
- Plastic action figures of a black Jesus arm-wrestling Che Guevara (see **Che Guevara merchandise**).

- A monkey. With the head of Monkey.
- Something a bit Mexican.
- A baby's T-shirt bearing the slogan: 'I'm Such A Punky Baby – I've Only Gone And Cacked Meself'.
- Monkeys.

Of course, no one really wants this crap. But they get it anyway . . .

> EMMA: Here you go, Gran – happy birthday. I got you a T-shirt with 'Porn Star' printed on it.
> GRAN: Oh, cheers. By the way, I never liked you and your dad's not your real dad.

Knights of the realm

It's the 21st century and thus fairly safe to assume that we have reached the end of the Middle Ages – yet people are still being knighted. But most of them don't even have any armour and can't ride horses at all, let alone well enough to do jousting. They don't even get together round a round table. The only way this concept could mean anything is if, next time there's a war, Mick Jagger and David Frost led the charge. In fact, that would be really good for so very many reasons.

L

Lastminute.com

Not cheap, not even last minute. And what's the big deal about Martha Lane Fox becoming so rich? She was stinking rich anyway, so that's just easy.

Now there are lastminute shops – positioned in railway stations, exactly like normal travel and accommodation agents only, erm, more last minute. Not sure how exactly: maybe they talk quicker?

Meanwhile, back on the website, they're auctioning TVs and fridges. Handy for all those last minute emergencies when you desperately need white goods in a goddam hurry and can only wait 28 days for delivery.

A lastminute online casino is also available – for all those last minute needs to spazz all your wages staying up till three losing at poker. Next year, they're introducing last minute penis enlargement.

Jessica Lever – Tory saviour

High on Adam Smith, at the tender age of 17 Jessica Lever pitched up at the 2004 Tory conference and announced herself its latest saviour – when a young woman of her age could more usefully have been out stealing cars or tagging.

In media parlance, she 'did a William Hague'. But what made anyone think we need *another* William Hague? We've already clearly got *enough* William Hagues. I mean, we've already got one William Hague. And we've absolutely no fucking idea what to do with that one. So *another* William Hague is definitely entirely unnecessary. We're full up with William Hagues.

Jessica is the niece of monetarist free-marketeer and Thatcher guru Milton Friedman. For her 14th birthday, Uncle Milt gave her a copy of his book *Capitalism and Freedom*. Most ordinary kids would be, like, 'Yeah, cheers, Uncle, fucking great – what, Woolies out of X-Box games were they, you stingy shit?'

But no: Jessica – who wants to be the first female Chancellor of the Exchequer – found Milt's tract was about '[the] things I really believe in' such as 'laissez-faire, freedom of choice, freedom from the nanny state' and, of course, 'fucking the poor'. Except she possibly didn't say the last one.

Asked whether the Conservatives have shed their image as 'the nasty party', Jessica said: 'Well of course we have! The prospective parliamentary candidate for Watford is an Asian man and, anyway, we've always been very inclusive. Margaret Thatcher was the first female prime minister.' Ah, but where to begin?

As Jessica sees it, young people are a natural Tory constituency. 'In general, young people like to get on with their lives – they don't like being told what to do, either by teachers, parents or the government. So, of course, a less interventionist government, economically and socially, is going to appeal to them.' Ah, but where to begin?

Jessica is now the poster girl of a supposed Tory resurgence among young people. The Notting Hill Set is a 'thrusting' group of young Tory 'intellectuals' who no one outside the 'Westminster Village' has ever heard of, and hopefully never will. Conservative Future, meanwhile – the replacement for the Young Conservatives, which was shut down by Central Office for being obsessed with pre-emptive nuclear strikes against the Soviet Union, hanging and the legalisation of incest – is now the largest student political organisation in Britain. This is a measure of how much Labour has alienated students (see **Former presidents of the NUS**) and is probably due to Tory opportunism in denouncing top-up fees, plus it's still pretty small at 15,000 members – but still, fucking hell, watch out.

Certainly, Jessica is pretty serious. Her every move at the 2004 conference was monitored by a showbiz 'agent' and engineered for maximum publicity. That's why she was wearing that conspicuous school uniform – even though she was, quite clearly, not at school. So, that's some pretty deep evil right there. And what was she wearing for an interview with the *Observer* at the end of 2004? Oops, she did it again.

It's time for the right-thinking people of the silent majority to put a halt to all the rot. Jessica Lever must be stopped. We must stress, though, that we're not suggesting that when she gets to college some wag should plant drugs on her and then call the police. I hope that's clear.

Libraries, public

When Treharris Library, near Merthyr Tydfil, opened in 1909, a procession of thousands of local people carrying banners and flags marched through the village, in the rain, to the new library.

Once Alderman Andrew Wilson JP, a local councillor and Mayor of Merthyr, had opened the library with a golden key, they all steamed in. The crush at the library was so great that the lives of young babies in arms were judged to be at risk. So many ladies fainted in the crush that they had to close the gates.

All the internet terminals were gone in seconds and, frankly, even 10 minutes late and you'd have been waiting months for a Catherine Cookson.

If people marched down to their library now for a golden-key opening ceremony, they'd only end up having this conversation:

'Got this book?'

'No.'

'This one?'

'No. Got some old tapes by Be Bop Deluxe and The Finn Brothers . . . no, hang on . . . they're out.'

When Liberal MP William Ewart introduced his Public Libraries Bill in 1849, the Conservatives protested that the rate-paying middle and upper classes would be funding a service mainly used by the working classes. One Tory MP argued that the 'people have too much knowledge already: it was much easier to manage them 20 years ago; the more education people get the more difficult they are to manage'.

Luckily, given the state of the modern library system, there's no great danger of the populace becoming hideously overeducated or difficult to manage. Last year, the entire stock of one library in Taunton was found to consist of one six-year-old copy of *Gramophone* magazine. With most of the pages missing.

'Lifestyle' music compilations

Like all products with the word 'lifestyle' attached to them, these compilations are designed for people who have neither a life nor any style. What they say is: 'I do not know anything about music. Please, Clever Marketing People, target my demographic and tell me what you want me to like.'

Who thinks these things up, let alone buys them? Take the Elite Modelling Agency Compilation. As the name suggests, Elite would be useful if you needed a model: perhaps you are a fashion photographer, or have dropped something down the side of the fridge and can't reach it. It knows shit-all about music. Neither do *Elle* magazine or *Cosmopolitan*: *Cosmo* is known mainly for doing questionnaires about blowjobs, which are sometimes related to, but are essentially different from, music.

The Friends Reunited compilation was not only pointless but also tasteless, containing tracks such as 'I Want You Back' and 'D-I-V-O-R-C-E'.

Even Jamie Oliver got in on the act in the mid-90s with, if memory serves me right, *Cockernee Jamie's Pukka Sub-Indie Dadrock Shitfest* – but my memory has been known to play tricks.

Describing their extensive compilation series, Starbucks says you should 'Think of them as mixed tapes from a friend'. I prefer to think of them as mixed tapes from Beelzebub.

But don't settle for buying a contemporary off-the-peg lifestyle: why not buy a lifestyle from before you were born? The Biba compilation of 2004, *Champagne and Novocaine*, celebrated the 'counterculture' Kensington boutique of the same name from the late 60s/early 70s. The definitive word on Biba was made at the time by The Angry Brigade, a mental anarchist sect that blew up a Cabinet minister's house and the Ford factory at Dagenham:

IF YOU'RE NOT BUSY BEING BORN, YOU'RE BUSY
BUYING.

The future is ours. Life is so boring there is nothing to do
except spend all our wages on the latest skirt or shirt.

Brothers and sisters, what are your real desires? Sit in
the drugstore, look distant, empty, bored, drinking some
tasteless coffee? Or perhaps BLOW IT UP or BURN IT
DOWN. The only thing you can do with modern slave
houses – called boutiques – IS WRECK THEM. You can't
reform profit capitalism and inhumanity. Just KICK IT
TILL IT BREAKS. REVOLUTION.

Now, this is pretty hardcore. Particularly bearing in mind
that this communiqué was released just after they had blown
up the Biba store – that is, with a real bomb. Extreme measures, certainly, but imagine what they'd have done if they'd
come across lifestyle compilations. In fact, maybe they did
and have spent the last 30 years developing a nuclear capabil-
ity. Think on, Kitchens Direct.

Lists

1. *OK Computer*.
2. *The Bends*.
3. The Campari ads with Leonard Rossiter and Joan
   Collins.
4. Peter Cook.
5. Shepherd's pie.
6. Delboy . . .
7. . . . falling over.

8. The sax solo in *Baker Street*.
9. *Kramer vs Kramer*.
10. *The Bends*.
11. *Bohemian Rhapsody*.
12. *The Bends*.
13. The video for *Bohemian Rhapsody*.
14. *Captain Corelli*.
15. *Star Wars*.
16. *Minder*.
17. Mrs Mills.
18. Moomin Mama.
19. The Cars.
20. The otter.
21. Jesus Christ.
22. This certainly is an
23. easy way to
24. fill up the pages
25. and schedules
26. and that.
27. Stanley Baldwin.
28. Lake Titicaca.
29. *The Bends*.
30. *OK Computer*.
31. *The Bends*.
32. *The Bends*.
33. *The Bends*!
34. *OK Computer*.
35. Martin Luther King.
36. The Shining Path.
37. Diderot.
38. *Angels*.
39. The Forth Bridge.

40. *The Bends*.
41. *Godfather 3*
42. was crap.
43. But the first two
44. were not crap.
45. Did you know that?
46. I didn't.
47. Jesus.
48. Jesus Christ.
49. Jesus H. Christ.
50. Might it just be possible
51. to start producing more culture
52. instead of lazily cataloguing
53. stuff that everyone already knows about?
54. Daley Thompson.
55. Brian Blessed in *Flash Gordon*.
56. Help
57. I want to get off
58. but I can't.
59. *Get Carter*.
60. Flea.
61. Timothy Dalton in *Flash Gordon*.
62. No, really.
63. *The Bends*.
64. I'm serious.
65. Nasty Nick.
66. This is killing me.
67. The otter.
68. Sankey's Soap.
69. *The Bends*.
70. *Gone With The Wind*.
71. Peter Cook.

72. Peter Cook watching *Gone With The Wind*.
73. Might it be possible
74. to just be quiet for a bit?
75. Okay then, let's see about that.
76. Here goes . . .
77. . . .
78. . . .
79. . . .
80. That's better.
81. . . .
82. . . .
83. Pure bliss, actually.
84. . . .
85. . . .
86. . . .
87. . . .
88. No longer . . .
89. hearing the worthless bleatings . . .
90. of a moribund civilisation . . .
91. turning everything of worth . . .
92. and integrity . . .
93. into another turdy fucking list . . .
94. . . .
95. . . .
96. *Revolver*.
97. NO!
98. *Pet Sounds*.
99. NOOO!
100. Delboy falling over.

Literary Heritage industry, the

In Kent, every house built before 1900 is required *by law* to claim that Charles Dickens once lived there. No business is considered off-limits for association with Mr D: consider Broadstairs' curry house The Dickens In India. Because Dickens is, after all, best known for his love of spiced meats fresh from the tandoor. Indeed, the adjective 'Dickensian' actually means 'having turmeric stains down one's front'.

And Hardy Country? What frigging Hardy Country? Note to Tourist Board sign-makers: THERE IS NO SUCH PLACE AS 'WESSEX'. It's an imaginative realm which, if it existed, would presumably be full of blokes who brood, treat their wives like shit for years, until they die, and then decide they loved her after all, then brood some more, on cliffs, while having visions of her. And who'd want to go there on their holidays?

Swan of Avon? Bollocks. The Literary Heritage industry is just a means of selling cream teas and notebooks with embossed plastic covers to people who don't read many books. If you do wish to appreciate some classic literature, your first port of call should rarely be someone from the Tourist Board who mainly specialises in giving out incorrect information about bed and breakfast accommodation.

Even worse than pretending imaginary places exist are places that obsess about writers who came from there even though they hated the place and did one out of there as soon as possible. Every visible square inch of Dublin contains tributes to James Joyce and Samuel Beckett. But Beckett hated Dublin so much that his rare visits back there made him physically ill.

Joyce left for good in 1904, aged 22, and in his lifetime was denounced by the Irish authorities as a seditious pornographer. Today, you can't move for statues of him or characters from his books. Strangely, though, no statues or plaques commemorate the bit in *Ulysses* where Leopold Bloom fantasises about eating a prostitute's poo.

Live8

It was beautiful, man. And so simple! To think that all it took to change the world was just one kooky Scottish girl to bump into a gangly Cabinet adviser in a café, and then for him to take her to the G8, and for her to click her fingers in front of all the world's financial bosses and emote about the world's poor, and they all stop behaving like a global version of those homeowner loan-sharks who advertise on daytime telly. All it took was her gently chiding tones and the assembled big balls were turning to each other, eyes welling with warm tears, and deciding that African children will starve no more. Beautiful, man. I'm crying now, just thinking about it.

Oh no, hang on, that was *The Girl in the Café*, Richard Curtis's pre-Live8 TV movie – kind of a global poverty version of *Lost in Translation* made by the Children's Film Foundation.

Live8 was even more beautiful than Kelly McDonald saving the earth. Doves taking flight during U2's set; Madonna kissing an African woman (NOT in a Britney way). Keane. Beautiful, man. His Majesty Lord Bob Gandalf singing '(I Don't Like) Mondays' and stopping at the line about dying, just like he did at Live Aid, once again drawing a clever parallel between the plight of millions of Africans and the victims of a teenage girl spraying bullets around a school. Okay, that's not so beautiful, man. But just think: if only Madonna could kiss *all* the African women (NOT in a Britney way). That would solve it. That would solve everything.

Chris Martin telling us how anyone who is 'cynical' about the political efficacy of a load of billionaire musicians mumbling is actually just 'stupid'. Beautiful, man. Peter Mandelson getting rich socialite pal Sabrina Guinness to show him how to text in his name to say, hey, he's against poverty, too, on the weekend – even the European Commissioner for Trade feeling part of this beautiful day of protest about, erm, trade. All those celebs who really care, like Chris Moyles, Paris Hilton, Jeremy Clarkson, ligging it up down the front in the 'Golden Circle'. Why didn't anyone think of this before? You know, Greenpeace or someone: uniting the world by harnessing the might of the corporate jolly.

For one beautiful day, we were all against African poverty. 'Yes!' said the world's leaders, 'We're against African poverty too. We should certainly think about reducing the number of kids dying every second for want of clean water or a bowl of rice. We will. We will think about reducing the number of kids dying. By 2010, it will be done. By 2010, we will have thought about reducing the number of kids dying every second for want of clean water or a bowl of rice. Er . . . no rush is there?'

For all this, his Highness The Most Honourable Bob Gandalf OBE awarded the eight great men '10/10 on aid'. It was written: Sir Gandalf and Bono Vox (see **Vox, Bono**) had set out to save the world. And lo, the world had been saved. Even if it hadn't.

Bill Gates introducing Dido? Isn't that what the end of the world will look like?

Loft living

In the olden days, factories were for making stuff in. Poo! Smell-y! These days, factories have found their proper function: as places for executive tosspots to live in while feeling superior and self-regarding.

Welcome to the 'funky' world of 'loft living'. This is not, we must make emphatically clear, the same as living in the loft. Executive tosspots do not spend their leisure hours surrounded by Christmas decorations, broken train sets and fibreglass lagging that makes your arms itch. No, these lofts are 'funky artist spaces'. They're 'the ultimate in cool contemporary living'. Particularly if you have a 'cinema kitchen' (and who wouldn't want a 'cinema kitchen', if only they could work out what one was?) or a 'colourful shower pod'.

Loft living began in downtown New York in the 1950s with beatnik artists and writers with absurdly thick-rimmed glasses taking over vast, cheap spaces in disused factories and warehouses south of Houston Street. These pioneering types all decided: 'Walls are for squares! I'm gonna spend all day staring at this decomposing apple core from various points around my football pitch-sized abode.'

As the urbanspaces website explains: 'The loft offered not so much a style as an attitude. Something that would set you apart from the dull conformity of suburban living . . . The disciplined order of conventional living in specific rooms for each task was about to be eschewed for the romantic notion of the bohemian decadence of open space.'

The disciplined order of conventional living in specific rooms for each task? Balls to it.

Eventually, of course, all the bohos were driven out by developers. Nowadays, far from being the 'cheap alternative to more conventional housing', loft living is actually more expensive per square foot than pretty much any other form of living. Loft spaces now generally attract the kind of person whose primary art involves devaluing random foreign currencies with the medium of computer terminal and telephone line. The kind of person who makes the average attendee at a Nazi rally look fiercely individualistic and bohemian. This is apparently quite 'funky'.

But that's just the start. With everyone wanting to live in factories, the artist Michael Landy has started moving all the houses into art galleries (starting with moving his dad's house into Tate Britain, which really, really pissed off his dad). Meanwhile, all the art is being shunted into pubs and bars. (See **Pubs selling shit art**.) Gradually, the drinks-serving aspect of pubs will be farmed out to the remaining houses. This will increase the demand for houses – because we all like a drink, however colourful our 'shower pod' – and the whole crazy cycle starts again. Factories will start making stuff again, with burly overseers driving the loft-dwellers out of their lofts and on to the looms. South-East Asian economies will nosedive in the face of sweatshop imports from the UK. Britain will occupy India again which, after initial resistance, the UK populace will support as it brings down the price of curry, plus, everyone's got pubs in their houses so they're pissed all the time and really confused.

And what's 'funky' about that, then? Eh?

Low-carb potato

Today we know that carbohydrate is dangerous both morally and spiritually. Previously spuds were cursed with a sizeable carb content – they were famous for it. People used to say: 'Have some spuds, they're good for you. Spuds are full of carbs – which is a food group.'

But now researchers at the University of Florida have developed a new breed with 30% less carbs than the standard baking potato.

'When it comes to beautiful potatoes, this one is a real winner!' assured Chad Hutchinson, assistant professor of horticulture at UF's Institute of Food and Agricultural Sciences. He went on to eulogise its light yellow flesh and 'smooth, buff-colored skin'.

Now *that's* science.

Loyalty cards

I fucking love Sainsbury's, me. I'd die for that supermarket. Sainsbury's *über alles*!

It pays to be loyal. If you have both a Barclaycard and a Nectar card and use the credit card to buy £12,000 of Sainsbury's stuff, you get enough points for a baseball cap with the Nectar logo on it. You do have to pay postage, but that's only fair.

George Lucas

Obsessively secretive movie mogul George Lucas spent years up in his Skywalker Ranch (crazy name, crazy ranch) plotting the second trilogy of *Star Wars* films. The renowned filmmaker, who last made a decent film during the final years of the Carter presidency, would spend hours explaining to his minions how the first *Star Wars* film was actually not the first film but, in fact, simply the fourth episode of a 12-part saga.

There's a whole new back story concerning Anakin Skywalker that will show everything we already know in a new light. And there's a Rastafarian frog called Jar Jar Binks.

These new films, he would continue, would be far superior to those earlier works because they are 'digital'. George Lucas loves 'digital' – in the late 70s he was one of the first people ever to buy a digital watch (it could perform Beethoven's *Für Elise*, which used to drive everyone on *The Empire Strikes Back* set absolutely spare). In the 21st century, his prime mission has been to change worldwide cinema technology over from film to digital projection. The new *Star Wars* films, which history would see as his true masterworks, would display the first flowering of this innovation's awesome potential.

At some moments, after spending many hours in front of the bluescreen, he would become distracted and cackle: 'They laughed at *Howard the Duck*. A film about a duck called Howard? Don't be stupid, they said. And . . . well, maybe they were right. But this time! This time I'll show them all. These three films will define the landscape of the blockbuster in the early years of the 21st century. At last, Spielberg will be my bitch!

'What's that, you say? Someone who actually knows about making half-decent movies is doing *Lord of the Rings*? Yeah, well . . . Those guys haven't reckoned on Jar Jar. Ha! *And* I've got Christopher Lee . . . What? They've got Christopher Lee too? Oh . . .'

Sadly, George was so distracted by the awesome potential of CGI technology that he turned the most loved film franchise of all time into arse sandwich. This was partly because the CGI-designed Rastafarian frog Jar Jar Binks was seemingly based Jim Davidson's hilarious West Indian character Chalkie. Not only that, he also based the story on a script so bad that the actors found themselves physically unable to act 'excited' or even 'remotely unembarrassed' in front of the camera.

Amazingly, Lucas was the only prominent New Hollywood director not on drugs.

Lush, the soap shop

Here are some interesting facts about soap:

- The first soap-makers in England used tallow, made from cattle. (See, I told you this would be interesting.)
- Soap is believed to have been invented by the Gauls. They used it not on their bodies, but to keep their hair shiny and red (hence the popular children's book *Asterix the Ginger*). Soap-making began in this country in the 12th century.
- It's just fucking soap, so a soap shop, a whole shop just selling soap, is a fucking waste of everyone's time.
- King Louis XIV of France was said to have beheaded three soap-makers for making a bar which irritated his skin.
- Soap is mostly used in conjunction with other items, like shampoo and toothbrushes, which really you'd want to buy all in the one place, what with them being functional items; you really shouldn't spend too much time buying soap, what with there being more interesting things going on in the world like wars and the darts.
- Modern soaps are most likely to be detergents made from petroleum-based products.

- They don't even do soap on a rope! I checked!
- Soap is mentioned twice in the Bible, though it may be a generic term for all cleansing agents.
- According to an article in a copy of *Metro* I once found discarded on the London Underground, soap's not even the best thing for cleaning your skin anyway. It's cleansing milk or somesuch. Do you stock that, Lush? No, you fucking don't.

Luxury tat

Consumption of luxury tat is up. In the first five months of 2004 it was up 27.7% in the US and 56.2% in Hong Kong. Let us all be thankful that war in Iraq or any of that kind of nonsense didn't take people's minds off their urgent need for a $19,450 platinum Vertu mobile phone.

On London's fashionable Bond Street you can buy all manner of expensive cack including Gucci dog bowls and solid silver bottle caps for HP Sauce and Heinz Ketchup bottles. Combine this with the statistic that Japan accounts for a quarter of the world's consumption of luxury goods and we get this disturbing conclusion: Japanese people are putting ketchup on sushi and HP on noodles. Luxury? It's madness.

This luxury mania is particularly amazing when you consider that luxury goods are not, according to Gucci CEO Robert Polet, real products: 'The goods are secondary,' he told *Time* magazine, 'because first of all you buy into a brand . . . [Luxury brands] give people the opportunity to live the dream.'

This doesn't just apply to handbags, mind. Asked by *Time* about moving from Unilever, where he was in charge of frozen food, to Gucci, which does not as yet offer frozen mixed veg or chicken Kievs, Polet said: 'I didn't sell ice cream. I sold concepts. I sold worlds in which people consume ice cream, but I didn't sell a piece of vanilla with a chocolate topping on a stick.'

He bloody did, though.

Polet added: 'People want to belong to certain aspirational worlds. Now, you do it at different price points – somebody buys into this world with a handbag for $500 or $800. And somebody else buys herself a dress for $20,000. Both allow people to be part of the world that they are aspiring to.'

So, that's pretty cool: a world where it is 'chic' for people to aspire to live in a world that only exists inside their head mirroring the world of *Sex and the City* which is a fiction on their televisions and think they can reach this paradise by giving all their money to some bloke who used to hawk frozen peas – meanwhile, millions 'aspire' to clean drinking water and would happily swap a world in which people eat ice cream for one where their child can eat enough rice not to die in excruciating agony.

Apropos of nothing, by the way, the founder of Gucci was called Guccio Gucci. And that's true. Even better, his dad was called Gucci McGuccio Kajagoogoo Gucci. Okay, that's not true.

M

Mac junkies

'Oh, Macs are just so much better than PCs. The operating system is about 12 times faster and they're just so much more efficient in, ooh . . . so many ways.'

Are they? Are they really? And how the fuck would you know, when all you use it for is copying CDs and looking at porn? What you actually mean is: 'They look nice.'

The Mac junkie will also crap on without end about how Microsoft is a big nasty corporation. No shit? And Apple's what then – a workers' co-op? No, it's a smaller nasty corporation – which uses child labour and beats its workers, whom it pays in beans, with sticks (possibly).

Do you know what Apple employees call company chief Steve Jobs? I'll tell you: Big Jobs. Or Shitty Jobby Job-head. And that's true. Okay, it's not.

Management consultants

A flourishing sector of the business world that is employed, at very great expense, by managers in other businesses to explain how to manage – in particular, how best to cut costs.

Remarkably often, consultants' advice comes extremely close to that given by management consultant turned Enron

CEO Jeff Skilling* in 1997: 'Depopulate. Get rid of people. They gum up the works.'

But – and this is key – DO NOT get rid of any management consultants. Or you'll be really fucked.

* Currently indicted on charges of fraud and insider trading, Skilling recently petitioned for his trial to be moved away from Houston after a poll showed a third of area residents associated his name with negatives like 'pig', 'snake', 'economic terrorist' and the 'financial equivalent of an axe murderer'. Yes those are negatives, alright.

Managers' mind games

Football: it's a game of two minds. The managers' minds. Which is why every big game these days is prefaced with a fortnight to four months' worth of mind games, as opposing managers try to unnerve each other with a witty *bon mot* here or some *random nonsense* there.

Published examples include:

'It's Chelsea's turn to lose now!'

'Arsenal were a disgrace last time. The ref will keep an eye on them tomorrow I'm sure!'

'We're better than them and they're the world's worst bad losers.'

'Come on then, what are you going to do about it, you spawny shit?!?'

'His wife is a filthy slut and I have shagged her.'

The most oft-quoted mind game came in 1996, when Manchester United's Alex Ferguson supposedly out-psyched Kevin Keegan of Newcastle to gain the Premiership title. He did this by suggesting arch rivals Leeds, who Man Utd had just beaten, would not try very hard when they played Newcastle in a vital upcoming fixture. With just one 'outrageous' remark, Ferguson had broken Keegan in the head.

'He's gone down in my estimation and I will love it, just LOVE it, if we beat them,' chuntered little Kev infamously, a finger jabbing furiously, his decomposing brain bubbling out of every facial aperture.

Ferguson was instantly hailed a Machiavellian genius, whose mind game had been the deciding factor. However, this overlooks the fact that his gambit was facile and blatantly transparent; any sane person would simply have ignored it and calmly got on with his job: the pressured Keegan, though, had always been one step away from curling up in the foetal position. Plus, perhaps crucially, Man Utd were better at football.

Arsenal's appointment that same year of Arsène Wenger gave Ferguson a new debating partner. The Ferguson–Wenger dialectic has thrown up many fascinating theses and antitheses such as 'Ruud van Nistelrooy is a cheat' versus 'Arsenal are cheats', and subtle put-downs such as 'Arsène – huh-huh, it's like "arse"; your name has got "arse" in it'.

The 2004–5 season, with the arrival of Jose Mourinho at Chelsea, saw this old rivalry become three-way.

Fergie said Mourinho had 'a shit coat'.

But Mourinho said it was Italian and 'really good'.

Comprehensively rebuffed, Fergie sulked for a bit and then went back to picking on Wenger, whom he called 'a shitter'.

However, the obsessive media coverage of Arsenal–Man U–Chelsea meant the season's real humdinger of a mind game got largely overlooked. In January, on the eve of a West Bromwich Albion–Manchester City showdown, West Brom manager Bryan Robson (and this is true) said that Kevin Keegan, now the Man City manager, had copied his trademark

80s shaggy bubble-perm hairdo off Robson. He, Robson, had pioneered the Dulux dog as England striker look, not Keegan.

This was quite a cuss: 'You had a shit haircut – and you didn't even invent it yourself!' With this sort of voodoo going down, how could Man City possibly score more goals than West Brom?

Weirder still: in cussing Keegan's bad hair, Robson laid claim to having invented the bad hair. He was cussing *his own hair*! What could this mean? Certainly, if I were Keegan, I would have been very much on the back foot – like a small, timid child lost in the woods, only more so. West Brom won 2–0.

Nelson Mandela, people comparing themselves to

In a major interview with the *Guardian* to coincide with the publication of his autobiography, Bill Clinton revealed that what got him through the Lewinsky scandal and Starr inquiry was the example of Nelson Mandela – who had been in pretty much the same situation.

Clinton said: '[Mandela] told me he forgave his oppressors because if he didn't they would have destroyed him. He said: "They took the best years of my life. They abused me physically and mentally. They could take everything except my mind and heart. Those things I would have to give away and I decided not to give them away." And then he said, "Neither should you."'

Mandela got into his spot of trouble by fighting one of the most powerful and effective systems of oppression ever conceived, apartheid. Clinton got into his spot of trouble spunking on a young woman's dress.

Mandela was jailed for 27 years. Clinton was told off a bit.

Martha Stewart, speaking about her impending incarceration for insider dealing in 2004, said: 'I could do it. I'm a really good camper. I can sleep on the ground. There's many other good people that have gone to prison. Look at Nelson Mandela.'

Stewart's situation would indeed have been identical to Mandela's – if only Mandela had owned a business empire worth $800 million and been jailed for lying to investigators regarding a suspicious stock sale.

Actor Johnny Depp, meanwhile, was so miserable working on TV detective show *21 Jump Street* between 1987 and 1992 that he tried to get himself fired by pulling stunts such as (and this is true) setting fire to his underwear. Speaking years later about his heroic struggle, Depp said: 'I was like Mandela, man.'

How true. And what if Depp had not managed to break those manacles of oppression? There would have been no *Finding Neverland*. Altogether now: 'Free-ee, Joh-hn-nny De-epp! Free-ee, Joh-hn-nny De-epp!'

In the world of international celebrity, you don't need to have been imprisoned to stand comparison with Robben Island's most famous inmate. Or have any discernible beliefs. After all, in his brave fight for what was right, what exactly did Bill Clinton stand for? La la la. Clinton Clinton Clinton – Old Billy Clinton: what did Big Bill C, 42nd President of the US of A, stand for? Nope, nothing coming. Ah yes, that's right: blowing his saxophone, staying in power for a while, having his saxophone blown.

There is, though, one major similarity between Mandela and Clinton: they are both black. The writer Toni Morrison called Clinton 'the first black President of the United States'. He wasn't though, he's white – I've seen him on the telly. And it's a funny sort of 'black President' who, during the 1992 primaries, would fly back to Arkansas, where he was governor, to oversee the execution of brain-damaged black man Rickey Ray Rector simply to look tough on crime.

Maybe Toni Morrison just meant that he was really into hip-hop. Or that he likes saying the words: 'You go, girl!'

Manolo Blahniks as metaphorical tool

Many lifestyle journalists appear frightened to write more than two paragraphs of prose without dropping in a little mention of Manolo Blahnik shoes.

Since being mentioned every five minutes on *Sex and the City*, the world has become deeply aware of linguistic uses of the word 'Manolos'. Something can be described 'as sharp as the heel on my new pair of Manolos'. A task can be 'as easy as strapping on a pair of Manolos'. A tiny dog can be 'as much a fashion essential as a pair of Manolos'. One day soon, somebody will be moved to write: 'I looked in the mirror and realised that I hate myself in directly inverse proportion to how much I absolutely adore my new Manolo Blahniks!' Then, with a bit of luck, they'll stop writing dreck and fuck off somewhere else for a bit.

Incidentally, the Spanish-born shoe-designing godhead is himself very skilled at using language. Once asked to describe the worst feet imaginable, Blahnik said: 'Maybe in LA, a hobo in Jesus sandals, with long, black, round nails. I think this is what evil looks like.'

The ability to see evil in a homeless person's feet is surely another sign of this man's tremendous vision. Although it is surely to be hoped that he is never in the position of bringing trials to the International Criminal Court in The Hague. Imagine the potential backlog of cases that this might entail.

Wonder what he would make of Slobodan Milosevic's feet. More or less evil than a tramp's feet?

Meal kits

From those gleaming new stalls on London station concourses. So, nowadays, commuters can buy their din-dins in kit form . . . wow, this must be The Future! Or just really, really lazy.

Commuters spend, on average, three hours a day crapping on and on and on about how they spend another three hours a day travelling to and from work. Well, that's what happens when you live a hundred miles away from where you work: unless you've got a fucking time machine, you are going to spend a lot of time travelling to and from work, you dick.

Media studies

After three years studying 'the media', I must be a real expert in 'the media'. Can I have a job in 'the media' now, please? Vacuous tossers.

Men's magazine coverlines

Talking about his magazine in a recent interview, *Nuts* editor Phil Hilton claimed the 'cleverly formulated coverlines' were a 'unique selling point'. Above the article was pictured the cover of the latest issue. The lead coverline was a sentence of just two large, emboldened words: 'Abi' and 'Titmuss'. Yes, that is clever.

To be fair, though, pulling in readers (or 'readers') to *Nuts* and other Abi Tit-mags is a fine art. These titles somehow need to convince discerning young punters that this week's pisspoor pictures of underdressed women are not exactly identical to last week's. This time, they're so disgustingly enthralling that, on opening the bag, readers will instantly feel like pigs in shit. So they adopt coverlines like: 'Look out, lads! This one'll blow your socks off – no word of a lie!' (that's real) And: 'Try to keep it in your trousers till you get home – you'll be sore tomorrow!' (that isn't real, but could be). Incidentally, if any inspiration-starved editor wants to use the line 'This issue will make you issue in a tissue', they can have it.

The classier end of the men's mag spectrum has the trickier job of letting readers 'buy into' an aspirational brand that will keep them informed about shaving but also assure them that there are also juicy pics for tossing over. The highly sophisticated *Arena* magazine opts for coverlines like: 'Clothing Not Tolerated!' and 'Kiera Knightley: the shoot we've all been waiting for!'. Which conjures up disturbing images of numerous well-groomed young bucks forever adjusting their ties, all with their lives on hold, just dying to see photographs of Keira Knightley wearing slightly fewer clothes.

If you are such a person, you should try using the internet. Honestly! You won't know what hit you! You'll be flapping away from now till next Christmas.

Men's magazine pullquotes

The big, bold quotes extracted from interviews with young women to go alongside the pictures in men's magazines are 'cleverly formulated' too. The smuttier titles inevitably pick out lines like: 'I love my bum – it's great to hold on to' or 'Another woman? Sure, why not?!' or 'Yes, I definitely think the readers of your magazine would have a chance with me, I really do. I'm sure they're all fantastic lovers.'

In the more aspirational titles, when interviewing a bona fide respectable star like, say, Rachel Weisz, the interviewer will awkwardly throw in a quick question about doing nude scenes or having sex. The actress's world-weary, noncommittal answer – something like 'Well, okay . . . I guess you could say that I like sex . . .' or 'hmm, my breasts . . . whatever' – will be printed in 40-point bold curlicues to hopefully bolster the impression that she is opening up her darkest desires rather than absent-mindedly wondering about lunch.

It will only be a matter of time before these pullquotes are artfully constructed by extracting phrases from throughout the interview to say: 'Kissing . . . another woman . . . in a big pool . . . of mud . . . . is always something . . . . I've wanted to try . . . preferably being . . . watched by . . . your readers . . . with their . . . co . . . cks out.'

Mid-90s lads edging closer to their mid-90s

'Back when I was hanging out in the Groucho trying to convince two girls from *Hollyoaks* to have a threesome, if you told me I'd settle down and start a family, I'd have said, "No way, ya tossah! Not me! That game's for jerk-offs, yeah?"'

'Now I realise there's more to life than spending three days in Vegas casinos wazzed off your spunk on methedrine. I don't think I ever knew true happiness until I renovated a barn in Gloucestershire and got into Shaker furniture while looking into the eyes of my little Alfie.

'Remember the 90s? That was me.'

Mini Coopers advertising estate agents
How far do you think your pseudo-graffitied, pseudo-retro cack wagons are from the already hackneyed ideal of the cheeky swinging *Italian Job*?

This far?

Or   this far?

Kate Moss
In the event of a nuclear war, scientists predict that only one species is guaranteed to survive unscathed: Kate Moss. She'll be scouring the post-apocalyptic tundra, fag in hand, looking for the hippest smoking crater around, and wishing there was just one gossip columnist left alive to report glowingly on her whereabouts.

If she just wore clothes and left it there, that would be one thing. But no, people get her to do all sorts of completely unrelated activities – like singing. Even though it is hard to see how she is better suited to making music than, say, Marcus Trescothick.

With grim inevitability, news of her liaison with Pete Doherty was soon followed by reports that she had been laying down some backing vocals for Babyshambles' debut album. According to reports, he thought her vocals were so good he was considering writing a duet they could sing together.

Good vocals? Are you on crack? Oh.

Motorist, the, as oppressed group

There is one inalienable right of man – recognised as such from Ancient Greek philosophy through to the classic statements of liberal rights such as the US Constitution – that today is being repressed as never before, casting a shadow over all ye who believe in Liberty. I speak, of course, of the right to drive about in a car.

When the RAC call for 'a charter which safeguards motorists' rights' to protect the noble car-driver from Nazi measures like bus lanes and congestion charging, they are drawing on a rich tradition of political thought almost as old as man himself.

It was Aristotle who first invented the notion of 'pimping' one's 'ride'. 'These forks,' he wrote, in his *Politics*, 'are bitchin'.'

George Washington, first President of the United States, famously said: 'As Mankind becomes more liberal, they will be more apt to allow that all those who conduct themselves as worthy members of the community are equally entitled to the protections of civil government. I hope ever to see America among the foremost nations of justice and liberality. And of course to be porky and drive round in SUVs. That goes without saying.'

Our modern-day Thomas Paine is, of course, Jeremy Clarkson, who said: 'The whole country has gone mad. If people want to sit in a traffic jam on the M25 for two hours in the morning on their way to work, why should anyone stop them?'

'Why,' he added, 'are all these German lesbians trying to get me out of my car and on to a bike. Bikes are gay. And I'm not gay. Jeremy Clarkson? Gay? Gay I am not. Just look at the size of my car. Is that gay? No.' Okay, I made that bit up.

Some people argue that Clarkson is 'just a tosser'. They point out his hair and his 70s rock jeans-with-shirt-tucked-into-them look, and they mock. Look at him, these people say, just look at the gangly great streak of cack – rocking out to AC/DC's 'You Shook Me All Night Long' and Bachman Turner Overdrive. Can you imagine that great twat shaking you all night long? Fucking hell, no thanks. That is what these people say.

Moto service stations

Why are Moto so obsessed with their toilets? Visit one and you will be confronted with 'Loo of the Year' certificates. Their website, meanwhile, goes on about how they have 'the cleanest toilets on Britain's motorways'.

Operations Director Brian Lotts said: 'Our toilets are open around the clock, every day of the year and are used by nearly 3,500 people every single day, so keeping them clean and fresh is a mammoth task.'

The website, moto-way.com, also has a quiz question: 'How much loo paper is used in our facilities each year?'* These people are obsessed with toilets.

Is it because they have nothing else to crow about and are desperately trying to resist blurting out: 'Look, you know and

I know that if you're going up the motorway and you fancy a crap and a coffee, we've got you over a barrel. What are you doing to do? Go somewhere else? There isn't anywhere. Ha, ha, ha, ha, ha.'

Moto service stations usually house a Little Chef. What a glowing advertisement their logo is for a place selling fry-ups and ice cream: a fat bloke. They recently announced plans for a slimmer logo – quite literally a *little* chef.

Shouty Michelin-starred French chef Albert Roux protested, saying chefs should be fat as it shows they love their own food: 'I would invariably vote in favour of a fat chef. I would say he loves food therefore he must be a good chef – he looks well. The thin chef doesn't look well.'

So, we've learnt something new: Albert Roux is forever driving up and down motorways, eating in Little Chef and crapping in Moto. The fat freak.

* 'Thirty thousand miles! Enough to go around the world 1.25 times!' F-R-E-A-K-S.

Chris Moyles

On 23 May 2005, BBC staff went on strike over four thousand planned job cuts inflicted without union negotiation. Among those spotted crossing the picket line was Radio 1 breakfast DJ Chris Moyles. According to that day's *Evening Standard*, this plain-speaking man of the people told union officials: 'I'm going to be sympathetic to your strike on my show.'

It's very strange, but on his show that day Chris mainly talked about the Radio 1 team losing to Iron Maiden at the music industry's soccer tournament, the Soccer Six, before adding that 'there's something to be said for good-looking women . . . or even not so good-looking women, but tarty women, in a football kit'.

Later, he asked Rachel for her favourite Chelsea player and she replied it was 'a bit of a toss-up' between Terry and Lampard – which made Chris and Comedy Dave laugh in their trademark cheeky way. Then came the comedy version of Gwen Stefani's 'I Ain't No Holla Back Girl' called 'I Ain't Not Heaving That Girl' about having to move stuff round your girlfriend's flat which was . . . well, quite hellish, actually.

Maybe, amidst all the craziness, there lay a deeply coded message saying: 'Stop the non-negotiated job cut madness!' Maybe he never promised anything of the kind to union officials and they just made it up to look like they knew famous people. Maybe, with so much hilarity going off all around him, Chris simply forgot.

To be fair, even though I had gone to the trouble of downloading the show from the Radio 1 website, I couldn't bear to listen to more than half of it – so maybe the second half was a radio rally that culminated in Chappers leading everyone in a lusty rendition of 'The Internationale' before they all occupied Mark Thompson's office and set fire to mocked-up redundancy notices out the window.

Or maybe he's just a monumental shit-bin.

Moylesy!

Music sponsorship

In 2004, Britney Spears claimed that filming Pepsi's Gladiator/'We Will Rock You' ad with Beyoncé Knowles and Pink made her 'feel empowered' (the campaign slogan was 'Dare For More'). Later that year, Beyoncé told the *Independent* that having Destiny's Child's tour sponsored by McDonald's made them feel 'truly honoured'. Yes, that's McDonald's, not Barnardo's.

This is the Pop Star as Saira from *The Apprentice*, standing on street corners shouting: 'Oi! Buy this stuff! Hey, what are you doing? Didn't you hear me the first time? I said, BUY THIS FUCKING STUFF! I've got a right gob on me, I have.'

Music and big business have always been curious bed-fellows, but never before has the former positioned itself on the hard receiving end of things quite so readily. In 1997, when Mick Jagger really got the bandwagon rolling by jumping onstage showing off the new 'Rock 'N' Roll Collection' of tour sponsor Tommy Hilfiger, many fans audibly gagged. But such days are long gone.

Now the stigma of being a sell-out whore has almost completely disappeared, with even nominally 'non-corporate' indie bands operating on the principle, 'Well, everyone else is doing it . . .' Events like America's Music Upfront conference even let labels showcase forthcoming albums to corporations like Procter & Gamble, Samsung and Mercedes for use in future adverts. Co-organising the event, Atlantic chairman Jason Flom apologised to 'anyone in the ad industry who has been neglected in the past' saying: 'Target your brands with our bands!'

One group who might conceivably not need the money or exposure is U2; but in interviews around their silhouette/'Vertigo' iPod ads, the band hit new lows of twisted-logic obsequiousness. Adam Clayton called the union with Apple perfect 'synergy' and Bono called the iPod 'the most interesting art object since the electric guitar'. At a press conference unveiling iTunes for Windows, Bono appeared on videolink calling the new confluence between Microsoft and

Apple 'like the Pope of software meeting the Dalai Lama of integration' (don't you just love it when he says things like that? Not just that it's so appalling but that he clearly spent *ages* thinking it up).

U2's defence? Well, basically, the iPod is so self-evidently fab that not helping it dominate the market would just be churlish. Chewing over the knotty issues, perhaps not too effectively, Larry Mullen told the *NME*: 'It's about making it look like it's not about the money.'

If this cosy relationship really is so undemeaning, maybe Bono could consider jumping onstage wearing an iPod and phoning Steve Jobs to tell him how great iPods are before adding new lyrics to 'One' about how we get to carry each other's iPods?

That would be like the Dierdre Barlow of Messianic Twat-Rock meeting the Prince Rainier III of MP3-Playing Interface Alternatives. Or something.

'Must have', the phrase

Being told how to be hip by media planks is a constant feature of modern life. For its June 2005 issue, *Red* magazine promised '235 Must Have summer fashion accessories'. Must we really have 235 summer fashion accessories? Why did they think summer would last that long?

Seeing certain films is 'utterly essential' – with TV pundits saying things like 'this is Christian Bale's year, without a doubt'. Imagine having no doubts that this year, or any other year, is Christian Bale's year. What certainty!

'The FeONIC soundbug is a must have' I was once told by a TV 'items' expert, because it turns otherwise useless flat surfaces like walls into speakers. 'Flat and rigid surfaces'? Balls to them.

Such figures are portrayed as modern oracles peering into the misty water to somehow divine the future of thinking, being, buying. In reality, they've been sifting through a pile of press releases. Or, sometimes, looking stuff up on the internet.

'My life after . . .'

Before the age of celebrity, most would react to a painful split by staying under their bedclothes and, on re-emerging, looking distant and distracted like Agnetha in late-period Abba promos.

Thankfully, modern celebrities have now shown us the correct way to grieve over dead love: by regularly unloading into the Dictaphones of reporters for bottom-end weekly magazines about how many tears you have cried, how going to nightclubs only partially kills the pain, how your ex liked dressing up as a barrister and hanging from the banisters, how you will never watch *Hollyoaks* again, that kind of thing. At regular six-monthly intervals, you can join your public in 'Looking back at the split'. Which is weird. You can stage a 'joyful release' photo, like Nicole, or you can drip-feed details of your former partner's infidelities, like Jenn. At some point, someone will cotton on to the idea of getting all Darren Day's exes together for a conference. That'd be good.

If anyone is too distraught to talk, mum can always open up instead. In early 2005, *Reveal* ran an interview with Kerry's mum Sue headlined: 'Kerry Katona: I'll get over my breakdown for the sake of my babies'. Mum detailed how her daughter had suffered an acute nervous breakdown, how she appeared to choke on anything that passed her lips, how she suffered a severe 2 a.m. panic attack after having spent the evening at a Ronan Keating concert and how at one point she actually curled up like a baby with her mother in bed. All this, remember, for Brian fucking McFadden.

Finally, mum revealed to *Reveal* her one great wish for her daughter: 'I would love to see Kerry with someone like Dec from *I'm a Celebrity* . . .'

Isn't that sweet? I wish I had a mum like that.

N

Networking

The dark art of pretending to like people in order to advance one's own self – even though that self has precisely nothing to offer the world barring an extraordinary aptitude for self-advancement.

The so-called Queen of Networking is Carole Stone, who has a database of more than 20,000 'friends' among the 'great' and the 'good'. Each Christmas she invites a select bunch of them to an intimate soirée, generally keeping the number of guests down to around 1,500 to maintain that intimate, friendly vibe.

The author of books about crawling up the arses of the rich and famous – sorry, making some really great mates – Stone says things like 'I felt I had been a failure so far that morning, as I hadn't yet exchanged one business card' and 'Will I ever accept that it is possible to say no to an invitation and live?' So, not at all insecure, then.

When her first book, *Networking: The Art of Making Friends*, was published, Carole wrote: 'I can't resist rushing in and buying a copy whenever I'm passing a bookshop. I have to stop myself shouting: "It's me, Carole Stone, I'm the author!" as I hand over my £7.99.' So, not at all insecure, then.

She continued: 'And I'm doing all those naff things like ordering dozens of copies for myself and rereading the book in bed. Meanwhile I'm trying to fit in every promotional opportunity I'm offered. I have talked to any local radio station that will listen, agreed to speak at a literary lunch in North Yorkshire and I'm off to East Anglia at dawn for local television. Meanwhile, I've talked on the phone to *The Lady*, the Press Association and *Top Santé* magazine. I'm about to meet the London correspondent of the French daily *La Tribune* and I'm wildly clutching at straws to find an excuse that would make me eligible for a piece in *Cheshire Life*. I've had my hair done three times in as many days for photo shoots and now *Hello!* is on the phone – no money, but . . . I know I'll get withdrawal symptoms when I'm no longer in hourly contact with my publicist. I could get hooked on all this attention.' So, not at all insecure, then.

Who's weirdest, though – Carole for organising her bum-lick-fest parties, or the people who go to them? A couple of thousand of the great and good, and not one single one of them has got paralytic and started hurling abuse and food at the others.

Guests at the 2004 party included Peter York, Sir Peregrine Worsthorne and Gillian Shepherd – and no one hit any of them. Not even York. What's the fucking matter with these people?

Ross Noble

Surrealist founder André Breton described the movement's cause as being one of 'freedom and the transformation of man's consciousness'. This highly original art movement sought to thrust the subconscious world of madness, dreams and disorder into the world of uptight bourgeois normality.

Sometimes the results were irritating twaddle, but most was attempted in the spirit of humanity's struggle to understand itself.

So what do we learn about the contents of 'surreal' Ross Noble's head from his 'surreal' *oeuvre*? That a) there's not a lot in there, and b) it's not funny. Like a fish with a hat on wouldn't be funny. Or just, like, a man eating biscuits and that. In a hat.

Novelists writing about current affairs

Reading newspapers these days, you need some basic ground rules if you want to avoid the sudden urge to throw yourself through a window. One of the most important rules (at least of those that don't involve *Sun* 'Youth Correspondents') involves first scanning right down to the very end of the article. If you see there a little copyright symbol followed by the writer's name, either turn over the page or in fact drop the paper and run off into another room.

This is because, whether you've heard of them or not, the writer will be a Very Important Author. They don't usually do this sort of thing but, on this occasion, they have chosen to lower themselves from Mount Literature and walk among us. They have been touched by current events, touched in ways we normal people just wouldn't understand. There are children dying, we've all seen the pictures. But have we seen the real picture? The big picture? The picture that tells us what we're all really feeling? Probably not. After all, we're not pompous novelists straining for pseudo-profundity.

How would any of us have made sense of the horrors of the World Trade Center attacks if it hadn't been for the likes of

Salman Rushdie, Ian McEwan and Martin Amis telling us how horrible it all was? This was, without the slightest shadow of a doubt, exactly the right time for showboating prose.

Who could forget the opening lines in Amis's *Guardian* piece on 2003's Iraq War? 'We accept that there are legitimate *casus belli*: acts or situations "provoking or justifying war". The present debate feels off-centre, and faintly unreal, because the US or UK are going to war for a new set of reasons (which in this case do not cohere or even overlap). These new *casus belli* are a response to the accurate realisation that we have entered a distinct phase of history.'

So powerful! So readable! So succinct! So unclear whether he thought the war was a good or a bad thing! Imagine if his actual proper literary endeavours were as trite, jumped-up and egocentric and had such little connection with reality. Surely then we'd all stop buying them?

Oh, yes, that's right: they are. And we have.

Nu-snobbery

The poor are a right laugh: look, they don't have much money! Ha ha ha. But there's a downside, too: they sometimes have bad skin because they don't use the correct sea-salt based exfoliant scrubs, and they can be violent.

In Britain, of course, we have a long and proud tradition of despising the poor. Back in 1384, Chaucer was moved to write: 'Paupers? Ryghte bunche of queyntes.' In the 21st century, this tradition is looking almost absurdly healthy. In 2004, following the soaraway success of websites like ChavScum, ChavWorld and ChavTowns, virulent class hatred made it on to the bookshelves with titles like *Chav! A User's Guide to*

Britain's Ruling Class and *The Little Book of Chavs*. The once-trendy website Popbitch started selling T-shirts emblazoned with 'Pramface', a slogan that righteously rips into girls who, er, push prams.

There was definitely some confusion, though: chavs are 'skinny and underfed', but also 'obese from always eating McDonald's'. They are 'inherently racist', but also 'spawn multi-coloured babies'.

'They all dress the same!' roared the ruggedly individualist middle-class professionals. 'They buy crappy jewellery at Argos!' Instead of, say, another chain store in the same shopping centre that's marketed at People Like Us instead. The sites attacking chavs for their aggression and mindless bad language were questioned by a journalist at the *Independent*. One respondent told him to 'fuck off and die'.

The word 'chav' actually derives from the gypsy word 'chavo', meaning 'little lad', and has long been familiar slang in Surrey and Kent (it's even on Sham 69's anthem 'Hersham Boys'). Now, however, it has started to denote a louty canker at the heart of our nation. Message boards were rammed with missives like: 'Chavs unfortunately don't yet fall into the category of rodent and in effect cannot be bludgeoned to death under the guise of pest control. Darn!' Or: 'Do not be fooled by there [sic] Humanoid looks, they are of another race, mainly scum.' Ha ha! What an hilarious parody of Nazi propaganda! Cool!

Of course, the *Daily Mail* couldn't wait to get in on this raw, virile fun and wrote of disgusting women who 'pull their shoddily dyed hair back in that ultra-tight bun known as a council-house facelift'. I'd have thought that, as a general rule of thumb, if your prejudices match those of the *Daily Mail*, you might want to shoot yourself. Amazingly, sometimes middle-class people in regular employment swear loudly and hit people too. And, get this: some, even those working for the *Daily Mail*, are more obnoxious than words can express.

Even so, it's clearly enormously liberating to rant on about single mothers and lazy workers like some gout-ridden Victorian bishop who's been at the laudanum again. Let's hope that soon there are just two words on everyone's lips: 'work' and 'house'. Put 'em together and what have you got? A sensible and modern benefits policy, that's what!

O

Obituaries in the future

Scientists predict that, if the ratio of celebrities to everyone else continues increasing at the present rate, then by 2048 the size of *The Times* newspaper will have expanded to fill the average two-bedroom flat. The increased space will be needed to cover stories about all the new celebrities and also to report the deaths of the old ones: sadly, Jeremy Speke will not live forever and some poor sod will have to write his obituary.

The Paper of Record will presumably dedicate whole sections to obits for celebrities: celebrity carpenters, celebrity gardeners, celebrity dishwashers, all the entrants in all 16 series of *I'm a Celebrity . . . Get Me Out of Here!* (the 17th was cancelled after the one with the 'tache out of The Darkness was eaten by an alligator), celebrity newsagents, celebrity wig-makers, celebrity adult literacy tutors and Howard from the Halifax ads ('Increasingly Howard found that the only thing that gave him xtra was crack cocaine').

Celebrity obituary writers will prepare their own obituaries. Which is poignant, in a way.

Observational comedy

Standing on a stage. Making trite observations about everyday life. In a futile attempt to be funny. What's that all about? Have you seen that?

'Official sponsors' of sporting events

Mastercard, official sponsors of the World Cup 2006, received a lot of criticism for initially insisting that all ticket sales had to be done by extremely complicated bank transfers unless paid for by one, and only one, brand of credit card: Visa! Only joking – it was Mastercard.

Coke famously banned Pepsi products from events they sponsored. Now, you may ask what Coke are doing sponsoring sports anyway what with it making you really fat, but they've actually got quite a long tradition of sponsoring sporting events, having got behind the 1936 Olympics in Munich – aka The Nazi Olympics, the one where Hitler wanted to show off Aryan superiority. Coke were pretty chummy with the Nazis generally. Indeed, Coke-staple Fanta was invented by improvising with local ingredients when the German Coke plants ran out of cola syrup during the war: they loved pop, the Nazis.

Anyway, at least Coke could argue it's an 'energy' drink. What about Canon – the 'official photocopier' of the England squad for Euro 2004? So, in the run-up to a big game, do the lads do a lot of photocopying, then?

Sainsbury's sponsorship as 'official supermarket' of England at Euro 2004 proved somewhat controversial, sparking the so-called Nectargate scandal. Wayne Rooney kept getting his Nectar card swiped during his team-mates' transactions and saving up the points to buy sweets. Steven Gerrard was particularly irritated, having done a big shop just before the fateful quarter final against Portugal – only to see Rooney dive in and hoover up the points!

Gerrard had specifically selected items he wouldn't normally buy, because they were part of an extra points offer. He'd been saving his points for a digital clock-radio and was really quite annoyed about it all.

England crashed out of the tournament only hours later. So, in what sense Sainsbury's were 'helping' really is beyond me.

Jamie Oliver biopic, the

In early 2005, plans were revealed for a Hollywood biopic of Jamie Oliver centred on the opening of his restaurant Fifteen.

The mooted star was – an obvious choice really – Brad Pitt. (As Jamie Oliver, in case you're confused.)

Adopt dramatic voiceover tones: 'He was a chef. They were the public. He had annoyed them with his Mockney ads for Sainsbury's. Then came some kids who needed his help. Would he save the advertising contracts – I mean, the kids – in time? Jamie – at a cinema in Hell, from Friday.'

And then there's the Nigella biopic: 'She was a chef. He was in advertising. He bought crappy art. She made chocolate brownies. He said she was sexier than Marilyn Monroe. But she wasn't.'

The Rick Stein biopic: 'He was a chef. They were some fish.'

Opening ceremonies

Great international sporting events like the Olympics and the World Cup are designed to bring people across the world together, to realise briefly our underlying commonality. And the opening ceremonies do indeed unite all the corners of the world with the same thought: 'Just fucking get on with it.' And also: 'Where did they get all that material?'

Wherever the host nation, these gammy displays of national pride always look like a school special assembly with serious money to burn. But there are moments to cherish: there's the grandeur in Barry Davies's voice as he reads from the script: 'And now . . . here come the grape-pickers . . . in their traditional costume . . . picking their grapes . . . from the grapevines . . . on the hillsides.' Or there's his mute disbelief at the sight of Björk dressed as an ocean singing about sweat.

The transcendent opening ceremony moment of recent years occurred at the opening of the 2002 Winter Olympics at Bonneville when each country was introduced with a short rhyming couplet – in French and English. One particularly memorable example went: 'They come from a land that's long and hilly / Welcome to the gallant athletes from Chile.'

Opportunistic vicars

The average vicar rarely gets the chance to shine. He is nominally at the centre of the community, but in reality no one in the community gives a holy toss. So it is understandable that, when he hears on the local news that there's been a terrible house fire nearby, quick as a flash he's got the dog collar on, he's into the Micra and he's round to the blaze to put his arm round a distraught parishioner who can't be seen to push it off in front of the local news even though their immediate thought is, 'Fucking vicar'.

Sadly, the vicar does not occupy a role in the centre of the community. In normal times, the community tends to keep the vicar firmly on the edge of the community. So surely, in times of distress, the community would be better served by rallying around a figure who is genuinely at the centre of the community. Like the chirpiest checkout cashier at Tesco. Or the man who peddles drugs.

Organic consumer scams

If you buy organic produce from abroad, and the organic produce has been transported by plane, then that organic produce, far from being an in-touch-with-nature, straight-from-the-soil bundle of environmental goodness, will have probably burnt its own weight in aviation fuel to get here (as part of a larger consignment; you don't get kiwi fruits individually flying themselves here from New Zealand).

The ethical farming group Sustain analysed a sample basket of 26 imported organic goodies: they found it had travelled a distance equivalent to six times round the equator (150,000 miles), a journey that will have released as much CO_2 as a four-bedroom household cooking meals for eight months. But the supermarkets know that the little 'organic' sticker means more money for them, so they really could not care less about jetset comestibles.

It pains me to say it but, if you want to go organic, you might have to end up dealing with hippies. Farming is the only area of life where hippies are best. You never hear about hippy builders, say – oh, we got some hippies in to do the extension and they were really good.

For farming, though, I'm with the hippies: it's either them or you end up with subsidy-guzzling reactionaries who fuck foxes. That's the impression I get, anyway.

Oscars, the

Another year on and Hollywood's managed to turn out, what, maybe THREE decent films? That's right, give yourselves a big clap. Funny how you never seem to win awards in competitions not run by yourselves.

P

Paninis

Panini was once simply an Italian sticker company selling packets of footballers' dumpy faces from small boxes situated by the till in newsagents. Then they went into the cheese toastie market and really cleaned up.

They were so successful in fact that they overreached themselves and ran out of bread, so they started to make their cool, continental snacks out of cardboard instead. They also didn't have time to print the standard warning on the side of the packet: 'Do not under any circumstances heat this fucker to 200°C as that is hot enough to melt the inside of someone's head.'

In Milan, no one would serve you a Caesar salad panini straight from a lovingly sealed polythene bag that is now practically on fucking fire. Unless, for some reason, they hated your family. Hot leaves? Bubbling hot yellow sauce? This is not the Italian way. Breakfast paninis with scrambled egg? Balls to them.

Michael Parkinson

Here is a slice of classic Parky:

PARKINSON: You really are rather good, aren't you?

ASININE CELEBRITY: Yes, that's right! Ha ha!

PARKINSON: Marvellous. So, when did you realise you were so great?

ASININE CELEBRITY: Not really sure. Probably around the time of a tedious childhood anecdote.

PARKINSON: Marvellous. Would you like to come round my house and have some drinks?

ASININE CELEBRITY: Yes please. By the way, I just want to say that you're looking so good, Parky. It's Parky, everyone, look! Doesn't he look great? I can't believe I'm here! With Parky! On *Parky*!

PARKINSON: Marvellous. I'm from Yorkshire, you know.

Tony Parsons

'I do like many blokeish things – football, women, kung fu – but that doesn't stop me from being a loving dad, a sensitive partner, a considerate lover.'

Or a chemically pure example of a cockmonkey. What a guy!

Penis enlargement e-mails

Ca:nYo:uLea:veMeAl:one:I'mQu:iteH:ap:pyWit:hMyDi:ckThe Wa:yIt:Is:AndEv:enIfIWasn'tD:oYouRea:llyThi:nkI'dWant:It: ToGetC:utOpenBySo:meBa:sta:rdSpamme:rs?

Picture bylines

These pictures are useful in helping the reader identify with the person behind the word-processing document. These smart, thoughtful portraits convey the message that the newspaper is employing the intellectual elite and reassures the reader that the following text composed is not by someone who is ugly (and, Christ, nobody wants that).

The messages etched into their expressions convey a series of complex signifiers. This one has a faraway look, scarred but resolute, obscurely strengthened by experience. Like Rutger Hauer in *Blade Runner*, it says: 'I've seen things you people wouldn't believe . . . attack ships on fire off the shores of Orion . . .'

Here the writer arches their eyebrow. This is to physically, literally represent that they are arch and knowing. It is helpful for them to do this as you will be entirely unable to detect this from the text, which will be self-obsessed drivel.

Another nods their head downwards, coyly smirking up to the camera, saying, 'Betya wanna shag me, don'tcha? Don'tcha? Huh!?' Others, peering sideways over their shoulder with their eyelids half-closed, look wry and mocking and say: 'There's no one in the world more wry and mocking than yours truly – but don't worry, I'm self-mocking too!'

These looks are fine, but they do show a certain lack of imagination. Other expressions that are crying out for serious writers to adopt include:

'Hey kid, pull my finger . . .'

'Give me some crack. I demand to have some crack.'

'Go on, touch it.'

'Grrrrrrrrr. Yap! Yapyap! Grrrrrrrrrrrr.'

and

'Yeah – I'm Jackie!'

Once you begin appreciating the subtle layers of meaning in these pictures, you actually want more. What about the people who write the TV listings, telling you that *Flog It!* is on at 6.00 with the line saying 'The auction show comes to Derby.' Why doom those poor buggers forever to invisibility?

Harold Pinter's anti-war poetry

Bombs.
Children.
Bombs on children.

Big bombs.
On small children.
With children's faces.
And children's arms.
And children's hair.
And that.

Shitty shitty shit shit.
Shit.

Up your arse.

Shocked? You fucking.
Should be.

Yanks: all scum!
Israelis: all scum!
Israeli Yanks? Don't get me.

Fucking.

Started.

© Harold Fucking Pinter.

Plastic surgery for pets

Joke corner: 'My dog's got no nose.' 'Really?' 'Yes, I had it chopped off because I didn't like the way it looked.'

It's illegal in Britain, but cutting bits off your pet is all the rage Stateside with some California vets even pointing to potential health benefits. Dogs with floppy ears need them clipping because they are more prone to inflammation from the 'build-up of moisture' (oh, and they can't hear as well – but they don't know that). Docking a dog's tail is highly practical because, according to one American Kennel Club judge, 'people can't grab the tail'. No, not if it hasn't got one.

Dogs can even be debarked by removing two folds of tissue on either side of their larynx. When these folds come together, the standard dog makes that woofing noise we tend to associate with dogs. Whip his folds out and, when he goes to bark, he produces a whisper, like a bark heard far away, when (get this) he's still right next to you!

Obviously no one likes a mental non-stop barking dog, but a spooky whispering one that sounds like he's down the road doesn't feel like much of a step up.

Amanda Platell

Coming over here, stealing our jobs – as the Australian Platell often says of immigrants in her column in the British *Daily Mail*, or previously as the press officer of the British Tory Party. Weirdly, it's often very popular for journalists to adopt slightly fascistic vernacular when their position in any prospective master race is hardly assured.

In the *Star*, James Whale continually envisages wiping yobbish 'scum' off the streets. And yet, if a Travis Bickle-like rain were going to fall, it's hard to see how he'd escape the onslaught.

Jet-setting columnist Taki has claimed that 'the fuzz' always arrest 'anyone who does not look like a criminal, i.e., white, middle-class, well-dressed, polite Englishmen' while Britain is being held to ransom by 'ethnic minorities'. And he should know – he's a Greek.

More amazingly still, *Sun* editor Rebekah Wade is actually a Romanian asylum seeker who has been cunningly fleecing the system for years. Burn her!

Poledancing lessons

Sarah Davis, the managing director of PoleCats in Birmingham, was forced to abandon plans to run poledancing classes for youngsters of 12 years old and over after protests from child protection groups. Responding to these silly and oversensitive complaints, she said: 'Our aim was purely to provide a way to help kids keep fit and boost their confidence.'

Fucking killjoys. Poledancing's just a great way of working out – and it's fun! It's like pilates for women who think: 'Let's play at being sex workers!'

Britain's top poledancing teachers Polestars assure us: 'Lessons are for fun, not professional training. All classes are a man-free zone!' This is a grave disappointment to many women who were actually hoping to spend their leisure hours swinging about for the delectation of drunken businessmen jiggling their hands around in their suit-trouser pockets.

Now, Polish dancing lessons – they get you really fit. And they're in the EU now.

Politicians' 'sexual aura'

In 2003, Gordon Brown topped the *Erotic Review*'s top 25 list of male sexual icons: 'Gordon Brown represents the scheming anti-hero women find so attractive. They don't want bland hero figures like Blair – Brown's brooding malcontent is much sexier.'

Okay. And how much sexier exactly? Would you, for instance, want to see him wrestling in the nude? Light glistening off his oiled flesh? Is the Chancellor really the kind of man you're drawn to in the street? Sort of pallid and hefty like he sits eating white bread all day with the curtains drawn? If so, you're just mental.

And is he really sexier than Blair? Don't write the PM off as a repressed freak who probably only does it with the lights off. Interviewing him for *Saga* magazine, Valerie Grove wrote: 'He is every woman's favourite shape, six foot tall, good shoulders, lean hips, weighing just under 13 stone, less than he did 10 years ago.' Sorry, how desperate do you have to be to find Tony Blair sexy? Have you ever *seen* other men?

'Shagger' Norris? John Major!! John bloody-fucking Major!?!?! Are you even technically alive if you look at John

Major and think, 'Hey, stud-muffin, let's get it on!'???? Ah, but in the flesh, he's got that undeniable something. Biographer Penny Junor famously mooned about his 'knack of making you feel that, for that moment, you are the only person he is interested in talking to'. Sorry, but the idea of John Major zeroing in towards you and telling you he'll treat you like a laydee is simply revolting.

And really, what's so bleeding studdish about Bill Clinton? Granted, he's not got buckteeth or a goitre, but that doesn't mean he's someone you'd want to see in the buff, aroused. For the love of humanity, he looks like Swiss Toni! Actually, Clinton just *is* Swiss Toni.

When George Bush paraded about the deck of the SS *Abraham Lincoln* in a battle flight suit in May 2003 to pronounce the war in Iraq 'over', many descriptions came to mind. For most of us, 'hottie' probably wasn't one of them – although it was for some maniac from the *Wall Street Journal*. Meanwhile, Republican speechwriter Peggy Noonan said she half expected Bush to 'tear open his shirt and reveal the big S on his chest'. S for Shitty Shithead Shitforbrains, presumably.

In the 2004 US election, Bush and Kerry tried to target the key undecided constituency of single women voters with their 'sex appeal'. Surely they would both have been better served targeting 'people with goose fat where their brains should be', rather than conjuring up terrifying visions of them having a wet-trunks contest.

Something has really gone wrong with your attitudes to sex if you want to whisper sweet nothings to Oliver Letwin or suck off Peter Hain. What next? Pieces eulogising the blubbery intensity of John Prescott? Ah, but when you meet him . . .

Powerpoint

The Microsoft tool that encourages people to think and talk like fuckheads.

Prince Andrew

In 2003, the fourth in line to the throne decided to travel from London to a lunch engagement in Oxford by chartered helicopter at a cost to the taxpayer of £2,939. When faced with complaints about squandering the public purse, a Palace spokeswoman explained that reliability was paramount as the Oxford date was a state banquet in honour of Vladimir Putin. Sadly, 'setting out earlier' was, she continued, simply not possible as there was 'something he'd forgotten to do' and also 'something on the telly'.

Prince Andrew loves helicopters so much that, when no helicopter can be found for him, he scampers up and down the Palace corridors shouting: 'Mummy! Copter! Mummy! Copter!'

Private education, the new acceptability of

Amazingly, the early years of the 21st century saw an explosion in the number of children being sent to boarding school. In 2003, the Independent Schools Census reported a rise in numbers for the first time since records began. Even more amazingly – actually, it's fucking stupefying – this upturn could apparently be explained by two words: Harry Potter.

That's right. Parents were persuaded to ship little Amy off to a remote castle to be dunked in an icy river with some minor royals every morning to make a proper woman of her, after reading some books about a boarding school for magicians.

Now this raises serious questions about these parents' own education. Not to put too fine a point on it, Hogwarts – is – not – real. Your kids don't actually get to fly around on broomsticks. Aren't you too mental to have children?

For many a moderately minted parent, gone are the days when they might feel even remotely ashamed for helping propagate raging inequalities. So it's all very fashionable to send little Ben across town in his cap like he's some character out of Jennings. It's all about choice, you see. And they're choosing to say, 'Let my child within a mile of ordinary kids? You're having a laugh.'

Labour, despite spouting rhetoric to the contrary in opposition, have been very friendly to private schools, reneging on commitments to abolish both assisted places – a bit of Thatcherite social engineering that sees the state (that is, us) subsidise places at private schools for kids from low-income families – or the schools' charitable status, worth about £80 million a year to their budgets.

Sod equality, though, and check out the exam results. Children at private schools have a much better chance of getting into an 'elite' university, and are likely to get better A-level results. Strangely, they don't fare so well beyond that.

A study by Warwick University's Department of Economics found that, when private school pupils went to university, they were less likely to get a good degree than those from state schools. In fact, they had an 8% lower chance of getting a first or 2:1 than a former state school pupil with the same A-level grades. And, funnily enough, the more expensive the school, the worse your degree was likely to be. Although they did usually develop a fine under-standing of roots reggae.

Dick Davison of the Independent Schools Council responded, calling the study 'a bit of a cheap shot'. Can't have been that cheap, though. It probably took ages.

During one recent outburst, Prince Charles attacked the education system's desertion of The Basics. He claimed, albeit rather clumsily, that 'all the letters sent from my office I have to correct myself and that is because English is taught so bloody badly'. A journalist later found that, perhaps inevitably, his office was made up wholly of former public schoolies. He did find they excelled at having a strong sense of personal entitlement. And they all were, without doubt, 'a really good laugh'.

Inadvertently, Charlie ended up underlining how little it matters what type of degree you get or even whether you can spell good: if you went to the right school, you'll still probably find yourself running the world in one form or another. Hurrah!

Product, the word

'What products do you use?'

'Oh, you know . . . pens, ball bearings, all sorts.'

'No, I mean beauty products.'

'Oh, sorry. You needed to be more specific. And less of a fucking twat.'

Property ladder, the

A marvellous system that separates society into two camps: the smug and the damned.

Public conveniences, lack of

Thank God for McDonald's. As a pleasing bonus, when you relieve yourself in McDonald's without purchasing one of their special patties of death, you are quite literally taking the piss out of them. Actually, no – you're quite literally giving piss to them. Anyway, they don't like it.

Bookies are also very handy for a cheeky wiz. And pubs. Except the one I popped into in Manchester in 2001 where the burly landlord made me buy a lemonade on reappearance from the lav on pain of a punch in the face. The fat bastard.

Pubs playing 'mellow dance grooves'

Your local pub has had a facelift, a tasteful refurb to help move with the times and appeal to the well-groomed 'modern crowd', people who appreciate more of a 'bar vibe'. It's a loose and yet happening establishment that's 'really chilled' till around 8.30 p.m., full of 'hipsters' lounging on leather sofas eating monkfish; then the tempo steps up thanks to some cool, unobtrusive 'mellow dance grooves'.

Really, it's not even a 'pub' any more. After all, the word 'pub' is short for 'public house' which carries certain implications of 'a house that's open to the general public'. And that's simply not accurate any longer; since the refurb and introduction of 'mellow dance grooves', to get served here now you clearly need to be a card-carrying member of The Cunt Club.

And what's with that music? Sort of Latin housey, sort of 'nu-breaks', sort of 'music for fuckers', it's clearly made by the most self-satisfied musicians on the face of the planet (even including everyone who made acid jazz); people who wouldn't recognise a decent 'dance groove' if it came along and set fire to their stupid little beards. It's so vapid it barely exists but still manages to create just enough hubbub to have everyone shouting into each other's faces.

Who actually likes this stuff? Who buys it? You never see hit compilations called things like *Pure Tepid Beats For Yuppie Mongs 2005*. And yet, somehow, for today's vaguely moneyed, pseudo-hipster wankstain, this mediocre sound sucks them in like a tractor beam.

It doesn't make you want to dance; but that's okay, it's there for 'atmosphere'. Pubs developing a 'bar vibe' are very keen on 'atmosphere'. What would really improve the 'atmosphere' immeasurably, however, would be 30 or so of Genghis Khan's most blood-crazed warriors charging through the door on mighty steeds, disembowelling punters as they go. Some sort of population cull feels in order, anyway.

Pubs selling shit art

If someone produced good art which they planned to sell at a reasonable price, would they need to display it in a place where people habitually become drunk?

Q

'Quality' Hollywood movies

People often stereotype Hollywood as a machine always preying on our basest needs for violence, sex and glamour. It's not, though, sadly. It also tries being deep too, which, when it comes to making films, is something that is best left to the Europeans. Except the British.

These films can generally be spotted by any sign of the following: Sam Mendes; Jude Law doing an American accent; Kevin 'I love the theater best' Spacey; Spielberg and Hanks! Together again!; a 'normal' middle-American suburb where everything is not as it seems; Gwyneth Paltrow playing a famous poet; Nicole Kidman playing a famous author (with a big nose); lives being changed forever by a car accident; Anthony Minghella; and Sam Mendes and Anthony Minghella! Together again!

Having directed *Truly, Madly, Deeply*, *The English Patient* and *Cold Mountain*, Minghella should be crowned king of ersatz profundity/portentous schmaltz. So it was almost inevitable he was chosen to direct the 2005 New Labour election broadcast designed to show the deep love and understanding between Tony Blair and Gordon Brown. The script, as far as I recall, went as follows:

TB: I think we can agree, Gordon, that it's all about the little ones. Don't you think?

GB: Oh yes. Hur, hur . . .

TB: I mean, we can talk about all this other stuff, but really, it's the precious little children that we love, isn't it?

GB: Sure.

TB: You do love them too, don't you, Gordon?

GB: 'Course . . .

TB: Oh, I love the babies, Gordon, I bloody do . . . save the babies!

GB: . . . righto . . .

TB: All the special little ones, I mean.

GB: . . .

Queen musicals

Writer Ben Elton blamed *We Will Rock You*'s terrible reviews on Britain's pervasive 'tall poppy syndrome'. Yes, it could be that. Or it could be Britain's pervasive 'thinking Ben Elton is a premier fuckwit syndrome'.

Nevertheless, like everything else touched by the hand of Freddie, the show proved such a hit that, at the time of writing, Elton is currently pumping out a sequel that reprises the dynamite formula of the first – that is, laughably shoehorns a tranche of Queen favourites into a plot similar to a Yes concept album.

So, why are Queen still so adored by the British public? Do we subconsciously get them mixed up with our ruling monarch, the Queen? Or did that Nuremberg rally video for 'Radio Ga Ga' somehow hypnotise the massbrain into thinking their silly-bollocks music was good for all eternity?

Incidentally, the posters of *We Will Rock You* show the back of a cast member punching the air in mimicry of the sainted Mercury. This image prompts the question: how did Freddie manage to perform like that – punching the air, skipping around the whole stage and thrusting his crotch everywhere while also carrying on singing his opera-flavoured rock?

Hey . . . maybe, just maybe, it was at least partly thanks to all the massive pre-show lines of cocaine?

'I don't know where he gets all that energy from,' said Mum.

It's from the cocaine, Mum. Mainly the cocaine.

R

R&B ballads

That is not an album. That is somewhere in the region of one decent fast song followed by 30 tonnes of Disney-does-gospel-with-satin-sheets-in-hell mush with no discernible words except, 'Woh-oh-oh-oh-aaaaaahhh! Ooooooh! Oooaoaoaoaoaoaoa! Aaargh! Aaargh! Aargh! Yooo-hooo!'

And those aren't even real words. Rubbish, really.

Railway menu cards

The idea is to make you feel less like a big mug and more like a valued guest. Okay, it says, you've waited an hour for this train, and you only got a seat because it's the middle of the day – but, look, we'll give you crisps: here is a picture of a packet of crisps, to illustrate this amazing good fortune.

The glossily produced menu cards left on your table offer an intriguing array of cuisines including said Walker's Crisps, costing '£0.60', Twiglets also costing '£0.60', and Mars Bars – today, a mere '£0.50'. Freshly caught, too, I'll be bound. Mmm. More obscurely, there's also 'Gourmet Bread Products' – currently retailing 'from £3.00'. How chi-chi is that? Oh, it's just really bad sandwiches.

The whole clinking-trolley-full-of-snacks-as-restaurant

motif has not yet reached its fullest potential. In future, perhaps they should consider employing a *maître d'* figure to bring round a leather-bound list of delicacies with the words: 'As madam will see, the specials are sandwiche cheddar au pickle and an amazingly tiny tin of juice. The chef hand-picked the dry roasted peanuts himself this morning at a service station on the M6, and I can tell you the Mini Cheddars have that perfect balance between MSG cheesy flavouring and flour. Aperitif, anyone?'

Restaurants that levy charges for food you have not in fact ordered

Forcing your product on people unbidden then asking for cash is a practice beloved of squeegee merchants, drug dealers, loan sharks and restaurateurs, who possibly refer to the ruse as 'the old bread and olives one-two'. Before rubbing their hands together and cackling quietly. They may do this. I don't know.

Bread and olives are, let's not be churlish here, a fine combo. But, crucially, I may not actually want them. I may want something else. Like a tiny circular pastry case with serrated edges in which sits a dollop of indiscriminate puréed fish in mayonnaise and food colouring with the world's tiniest fragment of red pepper on top of it. Or chips.

And why stop there? Why not just slap a plate down on the table and announce: 'Venison sausages in redcurrant jus au mash with a side order of savoy cabbage: here you go. Oh, and I've ordered you this wine. It's nice. Anyway, I've opened it now, so sup up, pay up and piss off – there's a good soldier.'

And, as I say, I like bread and olives.

Restaurants with unfeasibly small toilets

As you squeeze between the door and sink into a cubicle that was last cleaned – that is, given a cursory wipe with a damp toilet roll – some time in the latter half of the 20th century, note how the extra table space in this Indian/greasy spoon/Chinese restaurant created by making the unfeasibly small toilet into which you are now trying to prise yourself so unfeasibly small is NEVER occupied by a diner. It will ALWAYS either be empty or occupied by restaurant staff smoking fags.

Sometimes these restaurants exude an air of genuine tragedy and thwarted ambition. This expresses itself in the need to walk a very long way to reach the unfeasibly small toilet. You must travel either upstairs or downstairs, through the never-used overflow room, full of piled-up tables once upon a time destined for stag do's and office Christmas parties that never came. These rooms often manage simultaneously to smell musty but also smell of paint, even though nothing that could rationally be described as 'decorating' has ever taken place there.

And there you are, in the semi-darkness, a bit pissed, whizzing your tits off on MSG, wading through this shrine to the Unknown Diner, this culinary purgatory, Godot's own bistro – just to piss in a cupboard.

Condoleezza Rice

Oil giant Chevron loves its former executive Condi Rice so much they named an oil tanker after her. How truly awful must you be for the oil industry to like you that much?

When news of this homage caused controversy, the

company quietly renamed the ship. The name they chose instead was *Condoleezza Rice? Oil-Loving Secretary Of State Who Oversees The Invasion Of Middle-Eastern Countries To Privatise Their Oil Infrastructure For Use By US Oil Giants? Never Heard Of Her! We Did Once Know Somebody Called Condoleezza Rice, But Not That One.*

Or it might have been the *Altair Voyager* – I can't remember now.

Everyone always goes on about Condoleezza Rice's supposed 'cleverness'. But she herself rates George W. Bush as 'someone of tremendous intellect' – so the bar has been set quite low here. Let's hope she never gets a job as, say, a GCSE examiner, because that could blow her mind.

Rice did attend the University of Denver at the age of 15 – but it was only to study the piano. And that is not, let's face it, a proper subject. Neither does it prepare you for high office: no one's going to look to Jools Holland in a crisis, are they?

Not unless it somehow involved boogie-woogie.

Rich, the

The sumptuous invitation cards read:

> 'From the château steeped in history,
> We enter a world of maharajahs and mystery,
> A gilded palace from Bikaner brings,
> A lavish feast fit for a king.'

The 'king' was steel magnate Lakshmi Mittal, the richest man in Britain and the third richest in the world. The 'château' was the finest in France, Vaux le Vicomte, on the banks of the

Seine. The 'lavish feast' was the June 2004 wedding of Mittal's daughter Vanisha, which lasted for six days. India's finest chefs were flown in, and Kylie Minogue performed; there was a live Bollywood extravaganza about the happy couple. Fireworks exploded in every direction, lighting up the whole of Paris.

The feast certainly was 'lavish'. Thirty million quids' worth of 'lavish'. I think the point they were trying to make was: 'We – let's not beat around the bush here – are the dog's very rich bollocks.' Mittal couldn't flaunt his wealth more if he flew over the poorer quarters of Mumbai in a helicopter shouting through a megaphone: 'You, yes you there – I am rich and you are poor. Look at me, up here, the rich bloke in the helicopter. Yes, me – Mr Moneybags here. Do not look at you, who is poor, look at me, who is rich.'

Fans of the rich, the kind of people who want to press their nose against the Mittals' glass and marvel at the shiny objects – people such as the author of the recent book *Rich Is Beautiful* – often invoke the so-called 'trickle-down effect', whereby the great wealth of a tiny minority, despite them apparently spending it on gilded palaces and lavish feasts, is quietly and invisibly percolating down to the rest of us. I'm not sure how: maybe they hide pound coins down the back of single mothers' sofas?

The rich are supposed to be useful and great and good. But, according to the 2005 *Sunday Times* Rich List, the five richest people in the country are:

5. Phillip Green (£4.85 billion). Owns a load of shops that are a lot like a load of other shops. So that's good. (See **Philip Green**.)
4. Hans Rausing (£4.95 billion). Invented the Tetra

Pak milk carton. Then fucked off from Sweden to the UK to (why, of course) pay less tax. Tossing milk cartons. Tremendous.

3. Duke of Westminster, the (£5.6 billion). Go-getting enough to be born absolutely stinking-filthy-rich. Puts the 'lord' into landlord. And also, come to think of it, the 'land'. To be fair, does let poor people live in his Mayfair properties for free. Not really.

2. Roman Abramovich (£7.5 billion). Russian oligarch. Pocketed Siberia's oil wealth. Got a shit haircut. (See **Football buyouts**.)

1. Lakshmi Mittal. Best known in Britain for slipping Tony Blair a few quid.* Worth a staggering £14.8 billion, having started with just the one humble steel plant. (Which was bought for him by his parents.)

Even the most cursory flick through the rest of the Rich List will see they're all fat, boring, self-serving bastards who no one's ever heard of – podgy old blokes from the City who are 'in finance'. And when you have heard of someone it's fucking Sting.

Either that, or it's aristocrats. There are 125 aristocrats in a list of 1,000 – or 12.5%. Of course, this just reflects the percentage of aristos in the population generally. Oh no, hang on.

Whether their blood is blue or red, the one thing that unites everyone in the Rich List is, of course, really, really, really hating tax. You'd think that as all the super-rich's super-riches are generated by the whole of society (and with the trickle-down effect turning out to be a little, well, 'inefficient') governments might risk slightly offending the delicate sensibilities of the rich by enquiring if, after all, they might like to, you know, pay some fucking tax?

Even a tiny increase would raise sums so large the Inland Revenue would run out of carrier bags to put it in. That way, the wealth could go directly into things like education, culture, healthcare, that sort of thing; steering it ever so slightly away from bank accounts in tax havens and sweetmeats for a clique of rapacious, parasitical, reductive, generally unpleasant shits.

If only it were that simple. Both Tony Blair and George Bush have found that, although clearly they'd love to tax the rich, it is a physical impossibility. Even if the rich didn't 'move abroad', there still wouldn't be any surplus billions heading towards society's coffers. Bush explained: 'The really rich people figure out how to dodge taxes.' Blair claimed that if top-rate tax were raised: 'Large numbers of those taxpayers – probably the wealthiest – would simply hire a whole lot of new accountants to do this and that.'

Compared to, say, using military might to recast entire societies in parts of the globe where everyone hates them, these two eminent men consider that closing a few tax loopholes would be 'too difficult'. Suicidal Jihadists? Bring 'em on.

Accountants? Accountants doing 'this and that'? To the boats! To the boats!

* Before the 2001 election, Mittal donated £125,000 to the Labour Party. Blair then wrote to the Romanian government persuading them to let Mittal buy a steel factory. Blair claimed it was a coincidence. But that was bollocks, wasn't it? Also, £125,000? With all that cash he's got? If I were a Labour fundraiser, I'd have said: 'Come on, you've missed a nought off that, you stingy cunt.' This is just one of the many reasons why I am not a Labour fundraiser.

Keith Richards

Keef is the original punk. The everlasting renegade pirate outlaw riffmeister. In a world of fakes, the Stones' legendary guitarist is the real deal, the keeper of the flame. Except, erm, he's a pampered old jetsetter and a very silly man.

The road of excess is meant to lead to the palace of wisdom. In Keef's case, it has led to the palace of tottering about playing the same riff for 30 years with a scarf tied round your head. Is that wisdom? Shouldn't have thought so.

But millions believe Keith has lived the rock 'n' roll dream so they don't have to. For them, personal nirvana would be to party with Keef back in the day. Even though partying with Keef back in the day would generally have involved watching someone fall asleep and drool and then wondering if he's started turning blue or if that's just the light.

The rock 'n' roll thing to say is that the Stones are 'his band', that Mick is just his singer. In which case, why does this renowned renegade let 'his band' tour the world sponsored by T-Mobile? Or cancel a string of UK dates because they were worried about paying more tax? That certainly doesn't sound very rock.

Keef is the fearless spirit who said: 'If you're going to kick authority in the teeth, you might as well use two feet.' But, in living memory, the only 'authority' Keith has kicked with two feet is The Ramblers' Association. In 2002, he won his long-running battle to move a footpath further away from his West Sussex mansion – even though it was already separated by a thick hedge and a moat.

Thankfully, Keith's lawyers took on the ramblers on his behalf. Nevertheless, Keith prides himself on being A Bit Tasty – and, to be fair, he is fairly dangerous. But only in that he's an addled old soak who insists on carrying concealed knives. While pissed.

During sessions for cobblers 1983 Stones album *Undercover Of The Night*, the guitarist would emphasise any point by swishing a swordstick. People said this was 'cool' when what they should have said was: 'Come on, Keith. Don't be such a twat all the time.'

Roadtanks – SUVs, 4x4s, etc.

Market researchers are good. The ones employed by the US car industry found that people who buy SUVs are insecure, anti-social fucks who couldn't give a beggar's testicle about their fellow man: and who'd have worked that out on their own?

Here's what Keith Bradsher of the *New York Times* reports the US auto industry says about 4x4 drivers: 'They tend to be people who are insecure and vain. They are frequently insecure about their marriages and uncomfortable about parenthood. They often lack confidence in their driving skills. Above all, they are apt to be self-centered and self-absorbed, with little interest in their neighbors and communities.' No way!?

If pushed, the head of General Motors would say they are 'right twats'. Probably. He'd certainly think it. Probably. And Humvees? Where I come from a Hummer is a really smelly fart – and I'm not driving round in one of those, not for all the tea in Tesco. Poo! No way!

4x4s are just a way of saying: 'My family's got a big cock.' They are a marvel of science and technology, though: when we were kids they only had 2x4s, and they were just pieces of wood. You couldn't off-road on them, not even in Chelsea. So things have certainly come on in leaps and bounds since then.

Amazing, science and technology, isn't it? Last Bonfire Night my girlfriend gave me toe warmers – they're little sticky gel packs you stick to the outside of your socks and – get this! – even though they are cold when you take them out of the packet, stick them to your socks and they go all hot and keep your feet toasty. Now, how does that work if not by sorcery? By science and technology, that's how. Or it could be sorcery. I don't actually know.

Royal parties

The fancy-dress party that Prince Harry attended dressed as a Nazi two weeks before memorials commemorating the liberation of Auschwitz had as the theme 'Colonials and Natives'. This is strange: have you ever been to a 'Colonials and Natives'-themed fancy-dress party? Have you even heard talk of a 'Colonials and Natives' party taking place somewhere in your town?

What's more, the 2003 fancy-dress party at Windsor that was gatecrashed by Aaron Barshak also had a colonial theme. So does the British royal family have 'Colonials and Natives' fancy-dress parties every couple of weeks or so?

Still, it must be nice reliving the glory days of Empire by cracking open the Pimms and feeling genetically superior. Maybe sometimes the Queen comes in dressed up as Queen Victoria. With Prince Philip at her side dressed as Prince Albert. Showing off his new Prince Albert.

Royals, the

All shit.

Well, except for Prince William who even I – a heterosexual male with strong anti-monarchist beliefs – have to admit to finding so unbelievably beautiful that I almost want to cry. Lord knows, I didn't want this to happen. But just look at him!

Sometimes, I actually find myself wondering whether it's love and start spinning involved romantic fantasies in which we both write each other poems and laugh and giggle and laugh some more.

Then, in my darker moments, I can't stop thinking about being taken roughly from behind by Prince Harry dressed as a Nazi.

Rude films

In 2005, adverts for the DVD of Michael Winterbottom's *9 Songs* featured the quote, in large capitals: 'THE MOST SEXUALLY EXPLICIT FILM IN THE HISTORY OF MAIN-STREAM BRITISH CINEMA – *THE GUARDIAN*'.

Clearly, the distributors had great faith in the reasons for the broadsheet-reading cinephile's reasons for seeing this film. And it had very little to do with the footage of Black Rebel Motorcycle Club.

Adverts for 2001 art-porn flick *Intimacy* read: 'YOU GET TO SEE MARK RYLANCE'S KNOB. NO, REALLY.'

For pseudo-arthouse *auteurs*, there is a new game in town: shooting a drearily pretentious film no one would ever want to see if it didn't have someone's real bits being inserted into someone else's real bits. Pretty soon, Danny Boyle will want to get in on the action, so watch out.

The appeal for the directors is obvious: they get to watch people having sex. They even get to order them about in the process. What the actors get out of the experience is less apparent.

Reviled actor-director Vincent Gallo's 2004 flop *Brown Bunny* famously featured a scene in which the actor-director is explicitly fellated by a character played by his ex-girlfriend Chloë Sevigny.

So how exactly did this happen? Maybe he phoned her up and said: 'Hi, this is your ex-boyfriend. The one with the cast-iron reputation for asshole-ism. Look, I'm not gonna mess you round, I'm gonna come straight out with it: basically, it's like this, baby . . . I want you to suck it on camera for this new thing I'm doing. Whaddya mean, is it justified? Woah, yeah! Course . . . I can't even believe you even asked me that. I'm outraged! I'm Vincent Gallo, important film director! What do you think? That I'd just ask you to suck it for cheap kicks or something? Man, that would be sick! So, anyway . . . that okay with you?'

In which incredibly strange world of strange fucking strange would the answer be 'yes'?

Donald Rumsfeld

When the Abu Ghraib pictures surfaced, US Defense Secretary Donald Rumsfeld told Congress that he and his staff were 'offended and outraged'. But it's kind of hard to see how he was even mildly surprised.

Certainly, I wouldn't have been very surprised if I was Donald Rumsfeld. Not if I knew the US intelligence community had long been intrigued by the possibility of sexually humiliating Arab males to extract information. Not if I'd helped set up a highly secretive Pentagon operation, sometimes called Copper Green, which, according to a CIA source speaking to *New Yorker* correspondent Seymour Hersh, responded only to the rules 'Grab whom you must. Do what you want'.

Not if I'd sanctioned General Miller to 'Gitmoize' the prison system in Iraq and extended the programme so far that army reservists, including what one official called 'recycled hillbillies from Cumberland, Maryland', were being used as prison guards. Certainly not if I knew that even the CIA (those drippy liberals) were finally holding up their hands and saying: 'No way. We signed up for the core program in Afghanistan – pre-approved for operations against high-value terrorist targets – and now you want to use it for cab-drivers, brothers-in-law, and people pulled off the streets.'

Personally, all things considered, I think that if I was Donald Rumsfeld and I'd heard that no one was being stripped naked and made to climb into human pyramids, I would have been absolutely fucking amazed.

But then, Donald Rumsfeld has highly refined powers of compartmentalisation. In fact, this skill has now become so advanced that sometimes his right leg can be kicking an Arab's head in while he himself is completely unaware of any violence taking place anywhere in the vicinity.

Then someone nearby points out: 'Hey man, look! You're kicking that Arab's head in!'

And when he looks down, he can't believe what he's seeing. 'Oh my God!' he says. 'That's terrible! Look at my leg kicking the Arab's head in! Jeez Louise!'

At this point, Donald Rumsfeld starts repeatedly shouting: 'You're going home in a fucking ambulance!'

To which he immediately responds: 'Oh my God! I'm so offended! My mouth just shouted the words, "You're going home in a fucking ambulance!" Can you believe this shit? It's outrageous! And offensive! I'm sickened to the very pit of my being by what I've just heard! Have you seen this Rumsfeld guy? Man alive!'

S

Arnold Schwarzenegger

- 3 July 2003, pre-campaign appearance in LA: 'I told you . . . I'll be baaack!'
- Summer 2003, campaign trail: 'By the time I'm through with this whole thing, I will not be known as The Terminator . . . I will be known as The Collectinator!'
- 14 September 2003: 'Davis and Bustamante . . . have terminated jobs. They have terminated growth. They have terminated dreams. It is time to terminate them!'
- 17 September 2003: 'I know that on 7 October, we will recall Gray Davis and say, "*Hasta la vista*, baby!"'
- 24 September 2003, during televised campaign debate to opponent Arianna Huffington: 'I just realised that I have a perfect part for you in *Terminator Four*!'
- 2 October 2003: 'When I get to Sacramento, I will immediately destroy the car tax. *Hasta la vista*, baby! To the car tax!'
- 31 August 2004, Republican National Convention: 'One of my movies was called *True Lies*! It's what the Democrats should have called their convention!'
- 31 August 2004, Republican National Convention: 'In one of the military hospitals I visited, I met a young guy who was in bad shape! He'd lost a leg, had a hole

in his stomach – his shoulder had been shot through . . . Do you know what he said to me? . . . He grinned at me and said, "Arnold . . . I'll be back!!"'

Did you see what he did there?

Self-examination columns

'Hmmm . . . have you noticed that no one eats avocados any more? Wow, think about it a second – it's true. That's amazing – no one eats avocados any more! We all decided at exactly the same time. Isn't that weird? Or maybe some people do eat them . . . they are still on sale in most places, after all. Anyway! Do you ever get a funny feeling in your left leg? Do you get that? . . .'

The essential skills of the modern columnist rarely overlap with old-style journalism. No more going outside and meeting people, checking facts or any of that passé nonsense – just make a big sandwich and start examining your own self. Go deep, because when exploring the self, you simply can't be too self-centred. There's no code of conduct to abuse when it's your own privacy you're invading. That would just be like abusing yourself.

But writers can't just write down whatever flickers across their consciousness. Okay, they can. But they also need a gimmick. One successful figure currently produces a weekly treatise focusing solely on their fingers. Going under the title Can You Digit?, a recent missive went: 'Hmmm. That nail needs cutting. Look, this one's growing faster than the one on the other hand. Unless I nibbled that one some time after I last cut them all . . .'

Another writer stepped up to the challenge with Fenced In, every week detailing the progress of the creosote they covered their garden fence with: 'I thought the bottom of the third panel needed recoating, but when I got closer I realised it was just the light. The fourth panel used to be the brownest one, but it's not any more. It still smells the way creosote usually smells. I quite like it. I know a lot of people don't, but I do.'

Then there was Everyone I've Ever Wanked About. This was followed up with Everyone I've Never Wanked About, which was bits of the phone book typed out. That column immediately boosted news- stand sales by an estimated 20,000 a week.

A competing title, inspired by such successes, employed another writer to explore the random sounds they could make with their mouths. Called Sounding Off, it started: 'Clickclickclick. That's nice. Babbety-babbety-babbety-bab. Not so sure about that. We're not getting anywhere here. I know – ratatatatatat! ratatatatatat! ratatatatatatat! Yes, I likes it!'

To bolster the now slightly passé fingers column, the original title decided to employ a writer who had no thoughts of any description whatsoever. Under the title Dry Brain In A Dry Season, its most recent entry went as follows . . .

'......................................what?.......................wait...............there was something... no......................it was nothing........'

Serving suggestions

Have the makers of hummus, say, *ever* received a letter complaining that there was no parsley included inside? 'The label clearly depicts a parsley garnish atop the tasty chickpea-based Greek dip. So where the shitting blazes is it, you robbing pack of thieving bastards? Is it customary for supermarkets wilfully to cheat their customers in this way?'

It seems extremely unlikely. Yet there are always two words found on every scrap of food packaging to guard against such an eventuality: serving suggestion. They may be small, but they're always there. Like people expect a jug of ice-cold milk to be included in their cereal packet. Even though that would represent a major spillage hazard – which nobody wants. Or a single cherry tomato in their pot of sour cream and onion dip.

The serving suggestions are not only dumb, they're woefully unoriginal. Readybrek is always – always! – served in a clean blue bowl. Why not, just once, show an illustration of the oaty cereal having been dished up into a bowl of another colour, or into another kind of receptacle altogether: like lots of tiny walnut shells or a pair of child's Wellington boots? Now *that's* a serving suggestion.

Sex tips

Some people are so expert at sex that they become 'sexperts'. Very much leaders in the field of how to use one's bits, these people inhabit a world of non-stop sensual erotica. They really know about genitals.

For any willing recipient of the awesome wisdom of a 'sexpert', 'sex tips' will inject your sex life with such unbridled naughtiness that any passing Bangkok whore would be moved to widen her overpainted eyelids with fearful fascination. Some of the most common 'sex tips' include the following:

- Breathe on each other. As one of you breathes out, the other breathes in, so you inhale each other's breath. Breathing – it rocks!
- Cover each other's legs in sealing wax. Hey, it's not for everyone but don't knock it till you've tried it. Waxy, isn't it?
- Don't underestimate the erotic potential of the elbow. Find out what you can do with yours and before long your love buddy will be dragging you upstairs as soon as you walk in the door.
- Lather up each other's pubic regions with shampoo and make amusing shapes. Laughter is a great way of creating a sexy atmosphere!?!?
- Stuff each other's mouths full of cheesy biscuits – then lick each other all over. You'll be amazed at the new sensations that you both experience.
- You'd be amazed how talking can get your partner feeling horny. Try reading aloud favourite passages from *The Aeneid*. Trust me . . . phew!
- During penetration, why don't you both imagine you are both soaring through the clouds on the wings of a giant swan? If either one of you can perform a convincing swan's call, so much the better!
- Oh . . . just, you know, new positions and that. Put your legs in funny places, that sort of thing.

Shopping centres, coach trips to

If you go on a coach trip to, for example, a market in Belgium, it will have nice cheese and stuff you can't get at home. If you go on a coach trip to a market town in the UK, you will at least see some of another town, and may pick up a bargain or two. If you go on a coach trip to Bluewater you will find that, amazingly, IT IS EXACTLY THE FUCKING SAME AS THE SHOPPING CENTRE NEAR WHERE YOU FUCKING LIVE. THE SHOPS ARE THE SAME. THEY SELL THE SAME STUFF FOR EXACTLY THE SAME AMOUNT OF MONEY. SHOPPING CENTRES ARE NOT REAL PLACES. YOU CANNOT MEANINGFULLY GO ON TRIPS TO THEM UNLESS YOU ARE A TOTAL FUCKING SHIT-FOR-BRAINS.

Shopping centres, names of

Going to a shopping centre is one of the single most painful things known to the sentient human. Calling the place Lakeside or Bluewater will not change that. It is not like being beside a lake. It is like being in hell. There is only one exception to this shopping centre name rule and that is Brent Cross – it's in Brent and it makes me feel psychotically aggrieved, so at least it's factual.

Shops that play shit music at ear-splitting volume

That's quite a nice shirt, I think I'll pop in there and try – oh, fuck, no I won't, they're playing Jamiroquai at 12 trillion decibels. Jesus, one of them's even dancing.

'Sir'/'Madam'

We supposedly inhabit an infinitely less deferential world, one where vicars and judges are not gods to whom we must offer unquestioning obedience but are human, just like the rest of us, only with silly uniforms and more money. Rather than referring to politicians as 'Mr Blair' or 'Mr Hain', people say things like 'dickhead' or 'you know, the smarmy orange one'. Given this, it's surprising how often you can find your-self, a lowly commoner, being called 'sir' or 'madam' like you're the Viceroy of India ordering high tea at the Ritz. Even though you're just in Blockbusters hiring a video. And one of the *Police Academy* series at that.

If I were to purchase some trousers, say, and were to approach the earnest bloke behind the till, we can surely pretty much consider each other equals; we could even exchange friendly pleasantries. But not when he calls me 'sir' like a scurvy-suffering rat-catcher addressing a dark-clad thane who's holding a broadsword to his skull.

But being a servile service culture square-bear really does-n't get you anywhere. Unfair though it may seem, when you call me 'sir', I am infinitely more inclined to call you 'knobend'. In reality, the only reason to call someone 'sir' is if they could cause permanent damage to your genitals if you didn't. Otherwise, don't bother.

Nigel Slater

As a frontispiece in his book *Real Food*, Britain's Greatest Ever Cookery Writer (Says Everyone) Nigel Slater declared: 'When I say butter, I mean unsalted; when I say salt, I mean Maldon sea salt; and, when I say sugar, I mean the golden unrefined stuff from Mauritius. Pepper is ground from a mill as I need it and not, absolutely not, bought ready-ground . . .'

What is it about New Britain's aspirational icons that they impart advice with this weird sense of barely concealed menace? As though not completely devoting yourself to Getting It Right – and possibly even just preferring sport and ciggies – might bring down more shame upon you than if you had shat the bed.

I was only wondering what to have for dinner. I wasn't planning on invoking the kind of wrath more usually found in the officer class of the 19th-century Royal Navy.

'Salted butter? Salted with salt that is not Maldon sea salt?! You, sir, are a *shit*! LASH HIM!! Lash him well . . .'

'Smart casual'

Workplace clothing policy devised by the Devil which decrees that suits are too smart and jeans are too casual. So what does that leave in the middle? Fucking chinos.

South Bank Show, the

In 2001, Melvyn Bragg rounded on BBC commissioners for dumbing down arts coverage with continual series about Rolf Harris's contribution to the history of art. The BBC filling its schedules with programmes about Rolf Harris's paintings was, he decided, 'a total dereliction of its public duty'.

Since then, *The South Bank Show* has continually demon-strated the way forward, showing how arts programmes should focus on important, serious cultural phenomena viewers may otherwise have missed – like The Darkness and the excellent paintings of Ronnie Wood out of The Rolling Stones.

Upcoming *South Bank Show* subjects include:

- *Flaneur moderne* Kate Thornton.
- Maverick prankster Dom Joly.
- Swiftian humorist Miles Kington.
- The Yakult 'friendly bacteria' ads.
- Video artist Abi Titmuss.

Still, it's got a good theme tune: de de de de de de de de – de! de! That's the end bit. De de de de de de de de de de, de de de de de de de de deee! That's the start bit.

Spam porn

'TODAY IS JIZZ DAY!' . . . Is it? Is it really?

Specimen cheques

'A personal loan from our highly reputable credit card arm could give you a helping hand for those moments in life when you need a little extra: remember last winter when the kids all demanded jet packs and you'd jizzed it all on elephant tusks and cockfights? As an existing customer, you're pre-approved to borrow up to £12,000. So we could soon be paying a cheque like the one enclosed into your account.'

And there it is – a cheque for 12,000 big ones. Okay, the word 'SPECIMEN' is stamped across it, but it's still a thrilling sight. And it's certainly a good job the company included this amazing document; if not for this fake cheque – featuring my own name! – I might not have fully appreciated the reality of the situation. Without that, I might simply have binned the fucker thinking it was more junk artfully designed to drag me up to my titties in debt.

Of course, the reverse includes a disclaimer: 'It is important that you make sure you do not take on more than you can afford . . . Banko Bastardos is a responsible lender . . .' But surely the inclusion of the specimen cheque implies that they're chasing the kind of person who not only has trouble managing their finances, but also has difficulty lifting a soup spoon to their mouth without scalding their ears. The sort of person who might shout: 'Hey honey, come look at this! All those zeros . . . this is an amazing thing that's happened to us here. These guys have chosen *us*!'

They're certainly not chasing people like Barclays chief executive Matt Barrett who, in November 2003, told the Commons Treasury Select Committee that he didn't use credit cards and advised his kids not to either, as they're a rip-off. As recorded in *Hansard*, Barrett said: 'Borrow on a credit card? What do you think I am – some sort of twat?'

Sponsored towns

Nothing induces civic pride like seeing your hometown covered in a blanket of signs reading 'This roundabout is brought to you by Comet' or 'These flower baskets come with deep love from Greggs the Bakers', the local park logo-ed up like downtown Tokyo during the sales.

As trains pull into East Croydon station, visitors are informed they have arrived at 'East Croydon – Home of

Nestle UK'. Because, clearly, Croydon's entire population is essentially subservient to the coffee-and-chocolate-and-stuff multinational many consider a world leader in the malnourishment of African children. So that's good.

Spotted!

Someone. Somewhere. Out. Doing stuff. Thanks for that.

Stand-up comedy routines of the 2020s

Do you remember Turkey Twizzlers?

'Star' journalists who write about lamps and bowls as if they were the Science Correspondent or Political Editor

In his play *Night and Day*, Tom Stoppard wrote: 'A foreign correspondent is someone who flies around from hotel to hotel and thinks that the most interesting thing about any story is the fact that he has arrived to cover it.'

Imagine being the same, only writing about coffee tables.

Stupid arguments for being paid too much for being on the telly

Gabby Logan once justified being paid in excess of a million pounds a day for what basically amounts to 'watching the football' by saying she sometimes has to react to the unexpected. What, like air traffic controllers and firefighters react to the unexpected? How unexpected does football get? Are the players going to spontaneously combust, or be beamed up into a passing Martian spacecraft? Shouldn't have thought so. Or is she going to be waiting for Chelsea to come on and 'Oh, hang on, orange strip? It's Dunfermline fecking Athletic! And they're – they're playing themselves!'

Newsreaders argue that wheelbarrows are required to pay them because reading the news is 'very difficult'. Now, I seem to manage it fairly well when I read the paper. I'd go as far as to call it 'easy'.

The worst shoddy excuses for minting it for doing nix are from people on breakfast radio/telly, who always use the argument 'We get up really early'. This is the reason that they are the third highest-paid occupational group, just behind milkmen and paper boys.

Subs' words

Sub-editors are the people employed to make journalists' copy clear and concise before it goes to print. They use words like 'blitzing', 'scorching', 'stunning' and 'searing'. You work it out.

They also like 'mouth-watering' and 'tantastic' – which is great because it rhymes with 'fantastic' but also includes the word 'tan'.

T

Tattoos

Weird military shows in which soldiers march up and down for a bit and then there's a dog display team. Used to be televised. (For the other sort of tattoo, see **Body art**.)

Sam Taylor-Wood

Sam Taylor-Wood is the ultimate New Britain artist; married to renowned dealer (art, not drugs) Jay Jopling, she has effortlessly combined being an ultra-relevant innovator in art with being a friend of Elton John.

Among the works that make important artist Sam Taylor-Wood – who, for one reason or another, features in virtually every weekend broadsheet ever printed ever – an important artist include: her film of David Beckham sleeping. That even sounds important, doesn't it? And the photographic series – inspired by 'early paintings of martyred saints with tears in their eyes' – of celebrities like Jude Law, Dustin Hoffman and Robbie Williams weeping on command. In whatever medium, the importance generally lies in providing self-obsessed people with the opportunity to be more self-obsessed than they already were. It's sort of a gift, really.

All this crying was, of course, a moving experience for all

concerned; Taylor-Wood would regularly go home feeling 'miserable', 'depressed' and 'intensely sad'. I don't know . . . being in a room with Jude Law crying his eyes out sounds like quite a giggle to me. But what do I know? I am not an artist.

Moving on to other forms of misery, Taylor-Wood began chronicling the desolation of America's Deep South. In an interview with Richard Cork in the *Saturday Times Magazine* (of course), she claimed that hitting the lonely road, with only a police officer for company and rubbing up against ordinary, horrendously unsuccessful Americans, was a profound, haunting experience: the blighted landscapes, the desolate shacks, the lost souls. 'I went back to London wanting to pare my life down,' she said. 'The poverty was scary and really, really frightening.'

Perusing the stark images laid out before her, she added: 'I've given some of these to Elton, to use on his next album cover.'

Either that, or he might just go with a picture of himself in a shiny suit eating cakes.

Later in the same article, Sam Taylor-Wood praised the Brazilian singer Caetano Veloso: 'He has such a fabulous *tristesse*, and I suppose my work is full of it.'

Yes, I suppose it is.

Techno trailers

Many TV production tools still cling to the notion that 'dropping some beats' over programme trailers will prick up young ears and get them flocking over. So trailers for David Starkey's *The Monarchy*, for instance, come backed with a pumping Detroit kick-drum pulse over which the renowned thinker/historian can be heard describing Henry II's despotic rule in almost perfect time with the beat. Yes, it's Ravey Davey

Gravey Starkey and he's invented a new hard-right-formerly-promiscuous-homosexual variant of hip-house.

Tennis parents

Human foetuses can't play tennis (not even if it's twins: where would they get the racquets from?). So a parent who decides their unborn child is going to be a tennis star has to be some kind of freaky freaking freak-nutter freaking freak.

Richard Williams, father of Venus and Serena, consulted psychiatrists about the best way to bring up children destined for sporting stardom. Possibly quite sensible, given their early promise on the tennis court. Except he did it before they were born. Freaky freaking freak-nutter freaking freak.

Melanie Molitor, mother of Martina Hingis, was so determined her unborn child would be a tennis star that she named her after Martina Navratilova. Still, that's better than calling her Boris. Or Goran. Or Pat Cash (Pat Cash Hingis – that's a shit name). Anyway, aged four, Martina was playing in tennis tournaments – as opposed to, say, with Sticklebricks.

So keen was Damir Dokic – father of Jelena – on dominating his daughter that he has found it very hard to let go. The right-wing nationalist Serbian ex-boxer made a name for himself by getting expelled from matches for hurling Serbian abuse at officials (which puts your dad's 'embarrassing' cardie in perspective). Perhaps wisely, his daughter expressed her gratitude by dumping him as manager and moving to a different country. He responded: 'She left us. We don't need her . . . She did things that she was not supposed to.'

And why tennis, anyway, which is shit? Why not mould your children to do something useful – like perfecting nuclear fusion, or playing the drums like Animal out of the Muppets? And those freaks who 'hothouse' their kids into genius mathematicians are no better. Hothouses are for growing tomatoes in. Is that what you want your child to be: a tomato? Freaky freaking freak-nutter freaking freaks.

Me, I believe the children are the future. Teach them well and let them lead the way; show them all the beauty they possess inside. Let the children's laughter remind us how we used to be. Actually, come to think of it, that's not me – that's Whitney Houston. Same difference.

Tesco

Is Tesco a state within a state waiting to take over Britain and run it as a quasi-fascist enterprise regulating every aspect of our lives?

The case for this proposition:

1. Tesco employs over twice as many people as the army – 237,000 to 110,000.
2. Not content with already pocketing £1 of every £8 spent in UK shops, Tesco is expanding its tentacles into every area of our lives – including insurance, online DVD rental and banking.
3. Tesco's colours are red, white and blue.

The case against:

1. It's a supermarket.

You decide.

ThankyouTony.com

More than 60,000 American citizens have clicked on this website and pledged their gratitude to Tony Blair for standing by the US where other countries faltered.

Site founder Jon Sanford of West Falmouth, Maryland, said: 'It seemed to me important that Americans said thank you to Prime Minister Tony Blair and the British people. When the call came to stand and be counted, the United Kingdom came to our side.'

Yes, but we didn't really want to. Most of us would have been more than happy not to have come to your side. He made us do it.

In fact, I can't think of many places I'd rather be less by the side of than Jon Sanford of West Falmouth, Maryland. Unless I was holding a megaphone and a stick.

I wonder if anyone's registered ThankyouTony. Thanksa fuckingbunch. Noreally,Ican'tthankyouenoughTonyforwrecking absolutelyeverything,youhugefuckingtwat.com?

Ticketing hotlines

'The bill for your £12.50 ticket comes to £26.99.' 'Great.'

Toast, overpriced

There's a lot of overpriced toast out there. Watch out.

Toto FM

Most radio stations in the land (swathes of Radio 2, London's Magic FM, all regional radio stations) appear to believe that modern music reached a climax in 1983 when a Los Angeles studio band called Toto laid down a little number called 'Africa'. What's going on here? Have Toto kidnapped their children? Are Toto masters of mind control?

At the time, few realised the song's pivotal importance in the story of modern music; most contemporary aficionados let themselves be distracted by lesser talents like Prince and The Smiths. Only a real seer would have been moved to declare: 'This music is so timeless, so uniquely powerful, that in the early years of the 21st century, people will still be hearing it as they browse around Curry's.

'Come on! The way singer David Paich glidingly fits the words 'Kilimanjaro', 'Olympus' and 'Serengeti' into one line – it's sublime. And that brooding, otherworldly soundscape . . . how it conjures all the energy and immensity of that most misunderstood of continents.'

Trade union leaders pretending to be hard

New Labour's rise to power left Old Skool trade union leaders with a case of the Emperor's new clothes (WARNING: do not dwell on this image – I just did and now can't get a nudey John Edmonds out of my head). After years spent telling their members (fuck it, now he's dancing) to wait for a Labour government to make everything peachy, here in Downing Street were (now he's having a shower – Jesus, why must this be happening to *me*?) a bunch of Thatcherite shitters taking their orders directly from The Man (ah, that's better – Bill Morris has just put a towel round him): 'Workers? What workers? You mean those people who clean my house? They look okay to me. What's the fucking problem?'

Union leaders were reduced to saying things like: 'Colleagues, when I said things could only get better, I meant, erm, a bit later on. I wouldn't exactly say there will be jam tomorrow. But certainly, one day, at an unspecified point in the future, there will be, in some unspecified quantity, some jam . . . or fruit preserve of some description, or an equivalent – it could even be honey – for some people, the identity of whom will become known later. Possibly. Of that, Brothers and Sisters, there can be no doubt.'

Amazingly, their members weren't overly impressed and started wondering what their glorious leaders did all day. Bungate – when MSF leader Roger Lyons was caught charging a 25p bun to his union credit card – gave them the answer: they sat around eating buns. Buns paid for by the members – quite literally, the fruit buns of their labours.

So some union memberships voted out the bun-eaters and turned instead to the so-called Awkward Squad – a bunch of Molotov-hurling desperadoes like Dave 'Knuckles' Prentis of UNISON, Billy 'Haymaker' Hayes of the CWU, Bob Crow-'bar' of the RMT, 'Handy' Andy Gilchrist of the FBU and Mad 'Frankie' Fraser.

The Awkward Squad immediately issued terrible threats to fight for workers' rights and to save the welfare state. Then they put some ambiguously worded motions into the Labour Party conference. Then they withdrew them. Grr! I'm telling you, these boys are fucking animals. They will stop at nothing. And they frequently do.

The Awkward Squad have variously done such dangerous and frankly awkward things as stopping the Iraq War being debated at the 2002 party conference – you know, the one just before the war. Or buried motions on PFI in return for vague and shady backroom commitments by Labour bigwigs to 'you know, generally be a bit nicer'. Strangely, though, this hardball strategy of occasionally mouthing off and then running away hasn't delivered the goods.

So, what now? Maybe train drivers' union ASLEF has inadvertently shown the way forward: during a disagreement over the direction of the union after Awkward Squad member Mick Rix* was replaced as General Secretary by union right-winger Shaun Brady, they took the time-honoured route favoured by the labour movement for generations: they held a barbecue. Then they all got pissed and had a big fight. None of that compositing motions then withdrawing them at the last minute or making gnomic remarks at conference fringe meetings. Just a good old-fashioned, bare-knuckle punch-up.

So maybe this is how the labour movement should deal with the government – invite them to a barbecue then leather the bastards. It'll be like *West Side Story* (in fact, I suggest you play the soundtrack from *West Side Story* to create a bit of atmos). Except this 'rumble' isn't over a girl, it's over the link between pensions and earnings.

Prescott, we know, has got a serious right hook so watch out for him. And Brown's a big fella, if out of shape. I suggest you first distract them with a table full of pies – then Bob Crow jumps on them from a wall.

Follow up with a swift jab to John Reid's goolies and setting fire to Peter Hain. Then give Blair the pasting of his life. But look out for Hoon – he's the sort of dirty bastard who might pack a blade.

This might seem a harsh and primitive way of dealing with the situation – but what's the alternative? Say you organised a big demonstration to kick-start a mass movement to save the welfare state. It might rain. And then what would happen? You might get wet. That's what. And who wants that?

Trends in interior design

Interiors magazines tell you that September is the month to:

- Decorate the walls with bird motifs.
- Discover the beauty of stained glass.
- Use summer's harvest produce to make jellies and chutneys.

No, it's not. It's the month to go to work/school/college, eat toast, drink too much, not get round to stuff and watch some telly. Rather like October. And November.

What do you mean you haven't repainted the whole house yet this week? Didn't you know that 'warm, vibrant and lively, orange is set to become next season's hottest colour'? Meaning that having a stylish house actually means having an orange house.

Until, that is, six months down the line when – with your house barely free of the smell of orange paint – the same homes mag wags its shitty little finger at you and says 'sophisticated, mellow and organic, sage green is set to become next season's hottest colour'.

What shall I do with my orange carpet? Burn the bastard in the street as punishment for it not being sage? My house looks like a fucking Tango commercial.

'New looks for table linen'? Shove them up your arse.

T-shirts, insanely expensive

The turnover for T-shirts in the UK economy is now greater than for all other commodities combined – including food and oil. This is due to the strategy of charging cackloads of money for them, even though, at the end of the day, they're only T-shirts that cost approximately jack fanny-adams to produce.

Not long ago, one could reasonably be expected to be an outcast from society for wearing a Donnington Monsters of Rock T-shirt. Not any more, though – not now they cost 70 quid. What about a fake-aged AC/DC T-shirt – a brand new T-shirt that looks like a faded eighties' tour T-shirt? A mere £69 (Selfridges, summer 2004). Or maybe a fake-aged Electric by The Cult T-shirt – a tad more expensive at £75 (because it's about 8.7% more ironic).

This desirable item is produced by a company called, ahem, Buddhist Punk. An iron law of insanely expensive T-shirts-making states that your company must have a silly name – a bit, you know, funky. (See **'Funky', the word, as applied to anything except a musical genre**.) Top marks here must go to the company Maharishi. Christ, if you're chump enough to give them 70 quid, you can't say they weren't advertising the fact they could see you coming. You couldn't give a much bigger clue short of calling your company Fakir. Or Snake-Oil. Or Skank.

Oh, but they've probably been also 'customised' (someone has added a bad print of Hong Kong Phooey or Michael Caine as Carter). Or even 'deconstructed' – that is, with seams on the outside, or bits of material added to, you know, consider the workings of your T-shirt and unpack its very, erm, T-shirt-ness. 'Deconstructed' T-shirts are the very apex of T-shirt design and are always – always – the work of major designers. M-A-J-O-R. People who don't just design T-shirts but also do, you know, trousers, and maybe even coats.

Please understand that these T-shirts are very expensive – anywhere up to 200 quid – because it takes a major talent to do this and only a major talent. Or a monkey. For fuck's sake.

TV bullies – 1

Telly is only entertaining when we're watching someone else's lifestyle being torn to shreds with the brutal, yet oddly humane, efficiency of Orwell's chief interrogator O'Brien.

Selling Houses presenter Andrew Winter treats people like dung because they have left stuff lying around their house. He can do this because he's the selling houses expert – he's been an estate agent since he was six months old and his evacuee's haircut implies that he knows about hardship, so you'd better listen up or you'll be living in this pit till the day you die.

'What's that computer doing in your living room?' he barks at someone who has, fairly absurdly, left a computer in their living room.

'I work there,' they whimper.

'Get it out, you silly git,' he responds, with genuine bitterness.

You Are What You Eat presenter Gillian McKeith, who has an old person's face but young person's hair, all but spits in her victims' fat faces. 'You're a heart attack waiting to happen, you should be ashamed of yourselves!' she squawks in her weird Glasgow-American accent, piercing them with her owl-on-speed eyes. 'What are your shits like? Diabolical, I'll wager.'

Supernanny Jo Frost has got so carried away with the Nietzschean implications of her calling that she dresses up like a Nazi dominatrix. It's a potent sight, but what kind of message does it send out to the kiddies? Maybe E4 should show *Supernanny Plus* in which she administers some light, after-hours whipping to a daddy who can't control his offspring.

What we need now is a single programme combining all the elements of ritual humiliation called *How Do You Fancy Having Your Psyche Rearranged, You Twat?* A City Academy Superhead could visit the homes of ordinary citizens and shout: 'Your hair is cack. Your house is puke. Your clothes are muck. Your kids are shit. You smell appalling. And I'm afraid, my dear, that you don't seem to know the first thing about making love. Here's a loaded pistol. Do the decent thing, there's a good soldier.'

TV bullies – 2

In 2004, the government commissioned an advert about bullying, featuring various sportspeople and TV celebrities saying things like 'I was the kid you pushed around in the playground': the intimation was – hey, if I'd been bullied at school I wouldn't be able to run so fast, so think on.

The advert featured Vernon Kay saying "I'm the person you destroyed for fun!' – to which any sane person is just going to say 'Cool. Where do you get these bullies – I'm going to get one'. So, a government ad *for* bullying. That's New Labour for you.

Two homes!

Increasingly, there's been an increase in the number of people who find it increasingly difficult to fit all their living requirements into one home. From the Cityboy's *pied-à-terre* in Tower Hamlets to the country toff's sprawling pile in Lincolnshire, Britain's second home craze is really hitting the roof. And, coincidentally, it's coinciding with the craze for everyone else not being able to find anywhere to live that they can even remotely afford.

The second-home market has actually doubled in the past six years, meaning our island now hosts 206,000 second homes worth around £40 billion (including 38,000 properties in London alone). We're turning into one big two-home wanker paradise! Some Cornish fishing villages have no homes for the fishermen to live in and no fish for them to fish due to depleted stocks. Well, boo-hoo for them because now there's a new show in town! One home? No! Get outta here! Two homes!

But there is a problem. A nagging feeling that won't be ignored. You've got your two homes. So have all your friends. But that fat City bonus won't spend itself and the Derbyshire Peaks are looking pretty tasty this time of year. What are you going to do? Come on, you know the answer . . .

Three homes! More than three homes! You prance around

like Louis XIV, anyway. Why not really go for it: buy a series of palaces and tour around with a retinue of food-tasters, violinists and elephants fanning you with palm fronds. A bit of a stretch financially? Get in touch with Kirstie and Phil – they've got a new series coming called *Relocation Relocation Relocation Relocation Relocation Relocation Relocation Tossbag*.

Two Jags

Come on, porky, you know it makes sense: Three Jags! Two Jags ain't not Jags enough for not no man.

U

Ubiquitous football sponsorship

Birmingham City sold sponsorship rights to stoppage time at St Andrews to the West Bromwich Building Society: their name gets read as the stoppage time is announced. You have to question the financial sense of the society, though – and not just for sponsoring one of the most boring teams in Britain: you're called West Bromwich Building Society and want to sponsor a team in the Birmingham area so people recognise your name. Hmm. I'd venture to suggest there's another Birmingham team that might fit the bill a tad more snugly. The one with the same name as your building society.

United Nations, the

See **Vox, Bono**.

Utilities competing for your custom

In 2004, watchdog body Energywatch received 40,000 complaints from baffled customers. Companies often stopped customers switching to competitors; salespeople regularly made false claims (I know!); bills didn't come for months, then all arrived at once; customers would find themselves circled by rustlers on steeds, whooping loudly. That kind of thing. Oh, and my particular favourite: people signed up to new suppliers thinking they were signing campaign petitions about the French.

Thankfully, the DTI and Ofgen have identified the culprit: it's not deregulation, which has caused prices everywhere to skyrocket, but us. We should shop around more. This, however, presupposes being able to read the small print on my bills without wanting to kill myself.

Signing up to a new supplier thinking you're signing a campaign petition about the French, though? That's quite stupid.

V

Villages, the concept of, in urban areas

Game of cricket on the green, anyone? Oh, there isn't one – just a three-lane arterial main road.

The term 'Urban Village' is used 'to describe a place in the city which has all the characteristics of a village'. Despite being in a huge urban conurbation sprawling off for miles in every direction you're simultaneously in a calming rural idyll. One notable countryside feature of the Holbeck Urban Village Partnership in Leeds, for example, is its massive network of Victorian factory buildings. Brixton Village in London is some council flats over the top of an indoor market next to a very busy road.

If you're standing in the middle of Ancoats in Manchester and, instead of being vaguely worried about being mugged in an alleyway between two disused 10-storey redbrick warehouses, you're thinking you're surrounded by shire horses, innkeepers stoking log fires and farmhands copping off with dainty lasses, you sure are some kind of visionary.

Basically, if the nearest cows come in reconstituted patty form, it's probably not a village.

Virgin Galactic

Virgin are already great. But they are about to get better: now they're going into space.

Richard Branson, who is like a cross between Nietzsche's Superman and Noel Edmonds, has promised space tourism to ordinary, everyday, stinking-rich citizens off the street within a few short years. He even envisages a string of hotels all orbiting the planet. Thanks to Virgin, humanity can finally embrace the cosmos. It's a glorious vision. They'll probably balls it all up, though.

Certainly, the omens aren't good. On 27 September 2004, the very day that Branson announced the deal with Mojave Aerospace Adventures – the firm behind SpaceShipOne, which left the atmosphere the previous June – the inaugural journey of Virgin's revolutionary tilting Pendolino train suffered a mechanical fault 25 miles after leaving Glasgow Central. After tottering along at 55 mph, the 85 passengers eventually had to change at Carlisle. Virgin called the glitch 'highly unusual'.

Clearly, Virgin like a challenge. So do I. But I also like not being torn into a million pieces in the upper atmosphere, and Virgin's experience of not letting that happen to anyone is, so far, not massive. There are loads of 'highly unusual' things that can happen in space, and the fact that there isn't any such thing as a replacement bus service 60 miles above the ground does, at the very least, give one a certain amount of pause for thought. If it all goes wrong and you end up drifting off into the void, listening to the freezing silence as the oxygen runs out, you'll find scant consolation in an amazingly small cup of complementary tea or coffee.

And even if everything does go to plan, there are other worries. For one thing, you could never be sure that, at some point during the excursion, when you peer out into the infinite void you wouldn't be blessed with the sight of Branson himself in a spacesuit tapping on the glass.

He would then point at himself and pull a grin that says: 'Yes! That's right! It's me! In *space*!'

And no one will hear you scream.

Volume of TV ads

Too loud.

Vox, Bono

In the run-up to Live8, Bono explained to the *Evening Standard* the full burden of his responsibilities: 'I represent a lot of people [in Africa] who have no voice at all . . . They haven't asked me to represent them. It's cheeky but I hope they're glad I do.'

Cheeky? Not a bit of it!

Previously, during the 50th anniversary celebrations of the United Nations, he explained exactly why the institution was so important: '[I] live off some of the statistics provided by [the UN] – it gives [me] the facts so that when I rant I have something to go on. Without Kofi Annan saying, "You have an open door at any time, Bono," I wouldn't have the same intelligence. You need to know what's happening on the ground.'

People often wonder what the UN is for. It is, we now discover, essentially a fact-finding service for Bono, the world's most important man, who has come here to save us, each and every one of us.

Bono is all around.

Tonight: thank God it's him, instead of you.

Washed and ready-to-eat vegetables

A fantastic way for supermarkets to turn a bag of carrots at 45.3p per kg into a bag of scrubbed carrot batons at £2.78 per kg.

Batons? Don't make me laugh. You couldn't run a relay race using anything of that size. You'd be almost certain to drop it during the changeover.

Water

If you are still drinking ordinary water, you must be some kind of freaking loser. I wouldn't drink ordinary water – bottled or tap – if you paid me, which, apart from anything else, would be quite a weird thing to do on your part. I only drink 'ultra-purified', 'restructured' Penta – 'the Choice of Champions'. Too fucking right it is.

This shit is scientific. Consider this blurb from the side of the bottle: 'Top athletes use Penta for ultimate performance.' Drinking this stuff makes you run faster: FACT.

'Busy mums and high-flyers use Penta to rise above the daily grind.' Anything endorsed by both athletes and mums – well, that's got to be some serious shit. Which it is.

High-flyers are usually right shitheads but, hey, they need

water too. And it's reassuring to know that when some tosspot in the City is bankrupting Guatemala, they're very, very hydrated and are therefore much more likely to piss their pants.

So, what's in it? Water! Yes, just freaking water – but more water than in old-fashioned water. That's right, there's more water per centilitre of my water than your Earthling water, you shit-water drinking fool. If you had 500 millilitres of your shitty water, and I had 500 millilitres of Penta, I'd have more water than you. Having trouble getting your brain round that? Try getting 'Bio-hydrated': it makes you alert, more intelligent and (oh yes!) more likely to cop off with fit people.

Not only is Penta 'easy to drink' (how difficult can water get – unless it's just been boiled in a kettle? But still, cool), it's also 'fast acting'. Because old water, while perfectly adequate for the Steam Age, is now just so frigging slow. If you've got broadband but still use taps, you're clearly some kind of chumpy monkey. So get with it, monkey chump.

In fact, the next time your local water authority comes knocking, demanding to know why you haven't paid the bill, tell them to shove their water up their arse, it's shit.

Weatherpeople's babytalk

The audience for most weather reports consists of particularly twee three-year-olds. This is why, if it's 'chilly out and about', the audience needs instructing to 'wrap up nice and warm'. If the sun's coming out to play, we should all be careful because its rays can be very strong. And if there's rain coming, the forecaster adopts a special pained expression: 'Naughty, *naughty* meteorological system!'

Okay, there might be a case for wincing slightly when relaying how another record has just been broken; that, thanks to the wonders of climate change, we have just witnessed the hottest February ever and Wales is aflame with burning bushes. But no, they get quite jolly over that sort of thing.

'Spits and spots of rain'? Fuck that.

Web portals

Judging by the homepages of AOL, Wanadoo and MSN, the internet is just one fucking massive, world-spanning copy of the *Daily Express*.

Chirpy presentation; perhaps a bit of news, although not much; asinine lifestyle tips, consumer articles that aren't really; sex tips; astrology (obviously); pictures of what's hot and what's not on the red carpet. Where are the conspiracy theories? The swirly graphics trying to sell you stuff? The good old-fashioned fully nude humping? Now *that's* the internet. At least you can read the *Express* in the bath.

Websites, superfluous

Surely the correct response to an ad for a new chocolate ice cream is either 'They look quite nice – I might buy one' or 'Nope, not for me' or total indifference. Not: 'Thank God they've set up a website about these ice creams, so I can find out more information before committing myself to such a significant purchase.'

At the cinema, on TV and in magazines, adverts for, say, new trainers direct you to a website solely dedicated to moving pictures of those self-same new trainers – presumably in case you haven't quite grasped the ramifications of the whole 'there are some new trainers on sale' message and need to research the issue further in the comfort of your own home.

Visit any of these sites and your screen will (assuming you've got the right plug-in) explode into a thousand swirling colours. For a brief moment, you'll be dazzled at how your crappy PC can contain such visions of kaleidoscopic wonder. Then you think: Why? Someone spent ages making that happen. Why?

Westminster Village, the

'So, Ms/Mr Important Political Journalist, have you been out researching stories about how power is affecting the populace?'

'No, but I've been to lunch with a figure whose name I can't mention! And, well, you wouldn't believe what they said about, er . . . thingy. Sorry, can't say. As you know, I'm quite an important figure in the Westminster Village.'

Weirdly, given that exam results keep on rising, the past decade has seen the number of 18–35-year-olds watching news fall by 9%. True, this is partly because some 18–35-year-olds can't be arsed. But it's also because the news is just full of phrases like 'the Westminster Village', which – as in 'the word in the Westminster Village tonight is' – actually translates directly into English as: 'This is some serious bollocks I'm talking right here.'

Other implied meanings include:

- The fact that journalists don't need to visit any places where people's lives are happening – unless, of course, Westminster Village politicians are going there too ('No, not a fucking HOSPITAL?!? There'd better be some fucking sandwiches . . .').

- How the reporter who gets told certain things over lunchy actually gets given a little badge saying: 'ME SO IMPORTANT, YOU NOT SO IMPORTANT'.
- The way any genuinely important issues are only relayed through a series of self-referential winks, tics and raised eyebrows – like the Jane Austen mating ritual only with more backstabbing shitters.

Wetherspoons

The writer Hilaire Belloc once said: 'When you have lost your inns, then you should drown yourselves, for you have lost the best of England.'

I bet Wetherspoons supremo Tim Martin – who has a mullet and is a major funder of UKIP – would like Hilaire: he was very pro-England and English tradition and all that, and he *really* hated the Germans. Belloc was bit, you know, French, but you can't have everything.

Oh, hang on, maybe by 'inns' he didn't mean cavernous identikit soul-vacuums hawking oven chips that look like the bar of a cross-Channel ferry after a nasty collision with a branch of DFS. Bellocs! Better drown yourself.

Meanwhile, if you really want to economise on booze, there must be better options than Wetherspoons: sitting on a park bench drinking Thunderbird, for instance. Or injecting yourself with cider. The latter option will probably kill you, but at least you won't be giving money to fucking UKIP.

See also: Hogshead, Yates's Shiteing Lodges, It's A Scream, Pitcher and Shit, All Bar Humanity, etc.

Robbie Williams

Robbie's autobiography is, of course, called *Feel*. Well, he'd have had some kind of chutzpah to call it *Think*.

Williams enjoyed writing his autobiography so much, he claimed to be working on a novel. He said: 'I have done most of the research. It's a very creative process.' Writing a novel a 'very creative process'? Yep, should have thought so.

We can here exclusively reveal the track-listing for his new album:

1. 'Catchy Yet Shit First Single'
2. 'Feel My Pain'
3. 'Love Me (I Am In Pain)'
4. 'It's Not All A Barrel Of Laughs Being A Famous Pop Star, You Know'
5. 'Bet You Hated My Guts When I Shouted "I'm Rich, Rich, Rich Beyond My Wildest Dreams!", But Actually I'm Just Like You. Only *Much* Richer'
6. 'America: I Love You'
7. 'America: Please Love Me'
8. 'Second Single No One Will Remember In Six Months' Time'
9. 'America: No, Really, Love Me. Love Me. LOVE ME!'
10. 'Not Being Popular in America is Really Quite Painful'

'Work hard/play hard'

I once saw a trailer for *Relocation Relocation Relocation* in which a bionically smug young professional couple said: 'We need our weekends to get over our weeks and need our weeks to get over our weekends.' So I watched the programme and, fuck me, they said it again!

They were right, though. Because their lifestyle did closely resemble that of Mötley Crüe in their mid-80s Sunset Strip prime. Rather than, say, a stupendously unquestioning twentysomething couple who frequent a few late licence bar-clubs after a week spent so far up their boss's arse they could clean the inside of his hat.

The general public is working longer hours, drinking more booze and snaffling more drugs than ever before (a recent survey discovered the average UK citizen now ingests more cocaine than a Colombian cartel boss dropping by on The Eagles in 1975). We work stupid hours and then relieve the stress by hammering our bodies with toxins, and – unlike, say, a Victorian chimney sweep whacked up on gin – we think this equates to radical high-living rather than just alternating between the twin modes of droney worker and droney consumer.

Soon, if New Britain gets any Newer, we will all be obliged to work and play so hard that the two will need to be combined. Young professionals will be standing around in All Bar One of an evening typing up reports on their palm pilots while chugging back bottles of Turning Leaf and eating Marlboro Lights. Young workers will conduct presentations from the middle of the dancefloor in Fabric, throwing shapes and Es in every direction and showing flow charts on a projector normally employed for 'psychedelic visuals'. Staff appraisals will be carried out in the ladies' toilets while racking out a line on the top of a filthy hand drier.

The offices, meanwhile, will have bars and fag machines and people from head office hanging round the leather-sofaed chill-out area whispering 'powder? Everyone will be living like Alan McGee at the height of his pre-breakdown Creation Records office 24-hour party drugathon.

This means that, before long, everyone will eventually crash out, go into rehab, come out and sign Hurricane #1. Which is a worry.

Wraps

A chicken wrap? With a lower half that's basically one massive reef knot of pitta dough? That actually admits on the packaging to containing just 20% chicken to 40% wrap? And that's 20% by weight meaning that, given the way that chicken weighs more than wrap, the chicken peeking out of the top is essentially all the chicken anyone is getting in this chicken pitta wrap? That is not, in any real sense, a wrap – in the sense of something being wrapped up in wrapping. That's just wrapping with some incidental stuff nearby, as if by coincidence rather than intent.

Healthy Option pitta wraps even make big claims to 'have less stuff in'. Don't fucking boast about it! Why not put a big sticker on saying: 'Now contains NO fucking stuff whatsoever!'

X

X&Y

The creation of Coldplay's epochal third album was riven with pain and strife. One version of the album was scrapped completely as the band decided to start again from scratch. During the tortured process, around 50 songs were junked to make way for the final selection.

So, what . . . there were 50 songs not as good as the ones on the final album?

Really? What, worse than that first one?

X, the letter, at the start of words where it isn't

You don't have to be Lynne Truss to be annoyed by this – and I'm not; I don't look anything like her.

Take that bastard Howard. He keeps asking: 'Who gives you xtra?' No one. No one gives you 'xtra'; there's no such fucking word. Get many points for it at Scrabble would you, Howard? No, you would not. It would be disallowed.

Or Virgin Megastore Xpress. What's even Express about it? It's just small: the staff don't fucking roller-skate around on coke, doing everything in a goddam hurry. Also, surely a smaller version of a 'Megastore' is just a 'store'? The 'mega' bit means it's a larger version of what you're calling a small version of a large version. Your basic unit here is a 'store' – which is what this is.

So if you think you're saving letters by dropping the 'e', you're actually using loads more than you need to because of all this other arrant nonsense. Branson: you want your fucking head looked at, man.

Y

YBAs – the biopic

How could anyone possibly make the amazing, soaraway story of the mid-90s 'BritArt explosion' even more deep and interesting and worthwhile than it already was? Well, you could turn it into a Hollywood film.

Amazing news: a big-shot producer behind *The Others* is indeed planning a Young British Artists biopic, to be co-produced with Damien Hirst, which is great because Damien Hirst's got a very impressive track record in film, having made the video for Blur's *Country House*, which was great.

<u>ACT I SCENE II. INT. NIGHT</u>

[*11.30 P.M., London, England. At their studio inside the top of the Big Ben tower, London, England,* THE CHAPMAN BROTHERS (*wearing traditional English artists' clothing of a smock and beret) are gluing model vaginas on to Airfix Messerschmitts.*]

DINOS CHAPMAN: I'm telling you, JC, it's got to be over a hundred.

JAKE CHAPMAN: It's fine. Ninety-two toy Nazi soldiers with cocks for ears is perfectly sufficient. It's your fault for putting them in the microwave.

DINOS CHAPMAN: And another thing: we're supposed to

be dark but hilarious conceptual artists – so why did you get Messerschmitts? You should have got Fokkers [*laugh track*]. The word Fokkers [*laugh track*] is intrinsically hilarious.

JAKE CHAPMAN: With the Messerschmitts you get a cool Nazi pilot with a grimacing face. Stick a cock on that and we'll have our own room in MoMa before you can—

[*Massive commotion as the door flies open and* DAMIEN HIRST *and* SARAH LUCAS *burst through brandishing machine guns. Both are sporting traditional English artists' clothing of a stripey top and beret.*]

DINOS CHAPMAN: What the fuck do you two want?

[*More commotion at the door as* TRACEY EMIN *falls through it, accidentally spraying machine-gun fire across the ceiling.*]

TRACEY EMIN: Ta-da!

[TRACEY EMIN *falls over.*]

DAMIEN HIRST: Jake, Dinos – the art-world needs us.

TRACEY EMIN: I'm pissed.

JAKE CHAPMAN: Gilbert and George can find their own fucking dog. I'm sick of it.

DAMIEN HIRST: It's more serious this time.

SARAH LUCAS: It's Saatchi.

TRACEY EMIN: I'm from Margate, you know.

DAMIEN HIRST: He's been sending minions out from his fortified island kingdom in a disused volcano on the Thames.

SARAH LUCAS: They've been buying up shit art that's a bit like ads only rude. They want to parade caged pseudo-subversive crappy artists like tame bears on the South Bank – in the old City Hall, where that bloke with the newts used to do, you know, the thing. It's a final assault from Thatcherism.

DINOS CHAPMAN: What are we gonna do – get down there and bust his ass?

DAMIEN HIRST: No – we're going to sell him a load of our shitty art and make huge vitrines-full of cash.

JAKE and DINOS CHAPMAN: Hurrah!

SARAH LUCAS: Do you want to see my melons?

TRACEY EMIN: Let's go for a drink.

[*Fade.*]

Yob crackdowns

In May 2005, Bluewater shopping centre famously banned youths from putting up their hoods indoors. This was helpful for a Labour government pondering how best to use its historic new third term. Suddenly, everything was clear: stop young people wearing leisurewear tops with hoods attached to the necks.

There are undoubtedly many complex reasons why some of society's less well-connected youngsters might feel quite surly. It's the sort of thing people write Ph.D.s about. Tony Blair, showing how real intellect works, blamed the parents. 'What I cannot do is raise someone's children for them,' he said, as though that would, in an ideal world, obviously have been the best solution.

Lovable Home Office minister Hazel Blears, really under-lining that the quest for cheap headlines was over, proposed that all young brutes doing community service could have big orange Guantanamo-style uniforms.

This idea had been briefly flirted with by the Tories in the early 90s, but soon discarded on realising the suits would become a street-style badge of honour.

Except there is one way that any potential outlaw appeal could be avoided: if, at all hours of the day and night, Hazel Blears also wears an orange boilersuit. If an orange boiler-suited Hazel Blears were, say, the subject of a 24-7 webcam broadcast, so the electorate knows she isn't cheating, that would surely enable the yob crackdown to achieve its true potential in driving disrespect from our battered isles for good.

While we're in a blue-sky mood, another obvious solution to the problem of hoodies at Bluewater: ban fucking Bluewater.

Yummy mummies

Don't just lie there! It's been two hours since you've given birth. Get on that treadmill now. Or you're never going to 'snap right back' by the end of the frigging week.

Society expects! Or, at least, a certain part of vile London moneyed tosspot society expects. Before your newborn's first month, you must be playing *Bartok For Babies* while baking organic muesli bars in your 4x4. If you do not spend on your child in its first three months the same as the average yearly wage, then your child will be ugly and stupid. And who wants that?

The capital is now so crazed with the desire to produce 'alpha children' that some toddlers are even going to Japanese classes. One recent article reported that one two-year-old had reportedly been taught Roman numerals, French and Latin. At nursery, instead of mixing with other children, she just stood howling – possibly in disbelief at the quality of her peers' conjugation.

I wonder what's the Japanese for 'teenage nervous breakdown'.

Z

Benjamin Zephaniah

Many 21st-century office workers pass the hours spent in a room listening to someone spouting self-aggrandising bull-crap by playing the popular game Business Buzzword Bingo. Now fans of anti-Establishment/anti-colonial doggerel can join in the fun – with Benjamin Zephaniah Bingo. Points are awarded every time you hear the poet utter the following:

- 'OBE? No BE!'
- 'You know, I was a bad boy . . .'
- 'No way, Mrs Queen!'
- '. . . so they put me away in Prison!'
- 'Who turned down their OBE? Me! That's who! Me! Not you! Me!'
- 'Maybe you didn't know . . . but I've just come back from . . . AFF-REEEE-KAAAAAA!!!'
- 'Me? OBE? OBE? Me? Naaaaaaaah!'
- 'I would just like it to be known that I sincerely hope I will never ever be considered for the role of poet laureate. That is not the job for me. Did you get that? No poet laureate am I!'
- 'Oh yes, Mrs Queen, I'm so grateful. Not!'

Zion train, the

It still hasn't come.

Z-list celebrities as fuckwit pundits

Just before the 2005 general election, the *Guardian* had a news feature rounding up predictions of the result from sharp political minds like 'Steve Harley, lead singer of Cockney Rebel'.

'What will happen in the election?' we asked. 'If only we knew what Steve Harley of Cockney Rebel thought. He had a number one in 1975, you know. So clearly he's going to know about all this. It had an acoustic guitar solo.'

The *Independent* has gone one better and given a column to Tracey Emin. When not crapping on about how she had a hard time growing up in Margate, her mum or her cat, Emin squeezes in passing mentions of current affairs, such as the question 'I'd like to know how much has been spent on the war in Iraq . . . I wonder where you get information like that.'

In newspapers, Tracey; the people who are paid to write in the newspapers which people read in order to learn information make it their business to find these things out and tell us – otherwise what they are doing is WASTING EVERYONE'S FUCKING TIME.

Acknowledgements

Many thanks to: the other contributors, Scott, Joanna and particularly Dorian Lynskey, who also came up with the title; Geoff Harvey and Al O'Neill for helping with the proposal; Stuart and James at Liberty Bell; our ever-supportive editor Antonia Hodgson; Tamsyn Berryman, Sean Garrehy, Jessica Clark, Vanessa Neuling, Rebecca Gray and everyone else involved at Time Warner Books, particularly anyone who gave us lunch and/or biscuits.

* * * *

* AIRPORT PARKI

* TONY BLAIR * DAVID BO

NEVER GOT OVER TH

CHARGE EXCI

* THE CBI * CEL

MERCHANDISE * CHUR

* CITYBREAKS * CLASS

ABOUT THE CULTURE OI

CLOTH

* EXERCISE VIDE

MARKETING THEMSE

WARMING SCI

BUSINESSMEI

* HOTDESKS

* BORIS JOHNSON * KAB

LIVING * LOYALTY CARD

MOSS * NETWORKI

AFFAIRS * P

* THE PROPERT

GROOVES' * DONALD RU

EAR-SPLITTING VOLUME *

WRITE ABOUT LAMPS

CORRESPONDENT OR POL

* OVERPRICED

* BONO VOX * R